COL SHEKHAR ATTRI, SM (RETD)

GEN Z & THE CORPORATE REBOOT

What Gen Z Wants and How Leaders Can Scale

This is a work of nonfiction. The events and the incidents mentioned in the book are true and real. However, some names and characteristics have been changed, some events have been compressed, and some dialogues have been recreated.

First Edition: December 2025
Printed in India

Printed at: Gapmeta Ventures Pvt. Ltd., Navi Mumbai
Typeset in Adobe Garamond Pro

ISBN: 978-93-6070-720-0

Cover Design: Prajakta Sawant

STORYMIRROR
Stories that reflect you

Publisher: StoryMirror Infotech Pvt. Ltd.
Unit No-F/705, 7th Floor, Kailas Corporate Lounge,
Veer Savarkar Road, Vikhroli Park Site,
Vikhroli West, Mumbai-400079,
Maharashtra, India.

Web: storymirror.com
Facebook: @storymirror
Instagram: @storymirror
Twitter: @story_mirror
Contact Us: marketing@storymirror.com

PROLOGUE

Airports have always been my quiet thinking spaces. They are places where time feels suspended—where conversations overlap with flight announcements, where people sit between departures and arrivals, and where I, more often than not, find myself observing more than traveling.

One evening, as I sank into a lounge chair with my coffee, a senior executive settled down beside me. His tie was loosened, his phone still buzzing with half-read messages, and his face carried the fatigue of someone who had fought more meetings than miles that day. After a few polite exchanges, he sighed and said, almost as if continuing a conversation with himself, *"These Gen Z employees—you can't hold on to them. They join with fire in their eyes, but before you even remember their names, they're gone. Loyalty means nothing anymore."*

I smiled politely, but before I could respond, something across the lounge caught my attention. A young woman, maybe in her early twenties, sat cross-legged with her laptop open, earbuds in, and a phone call on speaker. Her voice was clear, sharp, and unwavering, *"I just can't work under a boss who doesn't listen. I need to grow, to try new things. If that means moving on, then maybe it's time. Or maybe I should just start my own thing."*

The executive beside me glanced at her too, shaking his head with a knowing smile that carried both disapproval and inevitability. For him, her words were confirmation of everything he had just said. For me, they sparked a thought I couldn't shake off. What he called disloyalty, she called clarity. What he saw as impatience, she felt as urgency. Two perspectives, sitting in the same lounge, breathing the same air, yet miles apart in meaning.

That moment lingered. It followed me into boardrooms and conference halls over the next few months, where conversations with leaders circled back to the same friction. Banking executives worried about attrition. Manufacturing heads complained about hierarchy clashes. Tech founders wrestled with the constant demand for feedback. Across industries, the pattern was unmistakable: this generation wasn't breaking rules for the sake of it—they were questioning the rules themselves.

I began jotting these encounters down, first in hurried notes on napkins and then in more deliberate reflections. Each interaction felt like peeling back another layer of the same onion—loyalty, hierarchy, feedback, boundaries, purpose, digital fluency, the itch to build something of their own. What started as one conversation in an airport lounge began to unfold as a map of tensions, insights, and experiments that revealed how the workplace itself was drifting.

This drift wasn't temporary, and it wasn't accidental. It was the new current of work. Leaders were being forced to let go of old anchors, while Gen Z was still learning to steer without capsizing the ship.

Recent studies reinforce what I witnessed in that lounge. One of them said that Gen Z workers expect to leave their current job within two years, while another reports that they are the least engaged generation at work, and only a few say they feel engaged on a daily basis. At the same time, another data reveals that Gen Z is the most entrepreneurial generation yet, with side hustles and new ventures growing twice as fast among them compared to Millennials.

This book is my attempt to capture that drift through real conversations and lived moments, not as a manual filled with instructions, but as a narrative that connects the dots between what leaders fear and what Gen Z demands.

Because sometimes, the future doesn't announce itself in strategy papers or policy memos. It reveals itself in the most ordinary of places—like overhearing a young woman in an airport lounge, reminding both of us, in her own way, that the rules of work have already begun to change.

TABLE OF CONTENTS

CHAPTER ONE

WELCOME TO THE SUMMIT

The idea that had first taken shape in an airport lounge was now standing in front of me in bricks, glass, and polished marble. The city's convention center, usually a home for industry expos and product launches, had been transformed for the next four days into something different: a neutral ground where two generations of workers would come face-to-face.

Banners lined the entrance: *"Leadership Summit"* Delegates were already trickling in, badges swinging from lanyards, phones in hand, half in conversation with the people around them and half lost in messages that kept lighting up their screens.

The lobby buzzed with the odd combination of corporate formality and youthful impatience. On one side, senior executives in suits lingered by the coffee counters, holding their paper cups like shields while exchanging cautious smiles. On the other hand, groups of twenty-somethings in sneakers and open-collar shirts clustered together, already filming short videos and posting stories: "Day 1 at the Summit. Let's see if they finally listen to us."

The auditorium doors opened with a soft hum, and I stepped inside. Rows of seats fanned out in a wide arc, tiered so that even the furthest row felt like part of the conversation. The stage was simple but intentional: a curved desk at the center for the three moderators, two sets of four chairs on either side; one for the Gen Z representatives, the other for the mid-level managers and behind them, a large screen waiting to display the day's agenda.

The air carried the nervous tension of a courtroom before the first case. Everyone knew they weren't here for speeches or polite networking. They were here for debate, for friction, for uncomfortable truths laid bare.

As the clock ticked toward ten, the seats began filling in. Executives with decades of experience sat shoulder to shoulder with recent college graduates, their conversations overlapping like mismatched soundtracks. A young attendee joked loudly about how this summit should have been on Discord, not in a hall; an older manager muttered something about how "respectful silence used to be the norm at events like this."

I found myself smiling. This was exactly the point. To put everyone in the same room, under the same roof, so that no one could scroll away, mute, or minimize the other.

At precisely ten, the lights dimmed, and a hush settled across the hall. A soft spotlight cut through the stage, illuminating the desk at the center. The screen behind flickered to life. The summit was about to begin.

The spotlight caught me as I walked toward the desk at the center of the stage. For a moment, the room blurred—the rows of expectant faces, the glow of phone screens, the soft shuffle of people settling into their seats. I gripped the edge of the desk, took a breath, and reminded myself why we were all here.

"Good morning, I am Nikhil Suri, and along with me I have Mrs. Kavita Nair and Mr. Rajat Mehra," I began, my voice echoing slightly against the high ceiling. A murmur of acknowledgement rippled across the hall.

"Airports," I continued, "are strange places for reflection. Flights land, flights depart, people rush in and out. But sometimes, in the noise, you overhear something that forces you to stop and think."

I could see heads tilt forward, curiosity sharpening. They'd heard fragments of this story before, perhaps, but not the whole of it.

"A few months ago, in an airport lounge, I was caught between two conversations. On my left, a senior executive was frustrated—he spoke about how Gen Z employees don't stay long enough to make an impact. On my right, a young professional was speaking just as passionately about her need to grow, to be heard, and to move on if those needs weren't met. For one, it was disloyalty. For the other, it was clarity."

I paused, scanning the room. Some of the older managers were already nodding in recognition. A few younger attendees smiled knowingly, as if they'd been in that very young woman's shoes.

"That moment stayed with me. I realized both sides had valid points, but neither side was listening to the other. And perhaps, that's the real problem. We don't have enough spaces where the two can truly hear each other. This summit," I said, spreading my hands wide, "is my attempt to create such a space."

The silence that followed wasn't uncomfortable. It was heavy with attention.

"Here's how the next four days will unfold," I explained. "We'll take the workplace tensions we all know: loyalty, hierarchy, feedback, work-life balance, purpose, digital communication, and entrepreneurship—and place them here on this stage. On one side, four Gen Z representatives. On the other hand, four mid-level managers. Behind them, all of you—our audience, our jury, our sounding board. At the end of every debate, you'll share your reactions. And I, well, I'll do my best to draw threads between the arguments, not to declare winners, but to find common ground."

I leaned forward slightly, letting my voice drop just a little. "This is not about proving one side right and the other wrong. This is about showing why both sides feel wronged and what lies between them. It will get uncomfortable, I can promise you that. But then again, growth never comes in comfort zones."

For a moment, I simply stood there, watching the faces in the hall. And then, slowly, the applause began—tentative at first, then swelling until it filled the room. It wasn't the polite applause of a corporate event. It was the applause of people who understood they were part of something unusual.

The summit had truly begun.

I glanced at the four chairs to my left, where the Gen Z representatives were seated. They looked equal parts eager and restless, the way students do just before an exam they've prepared for but not in the way the teacher expects.

"Let's start with introductions," I said, motioning to them. "Not just names, but what you stand for. Keep it brief, but keep it honest."

The first to rise was Aarav. Slim, sharp-eyed, with a smartwatch strapped firmly on his wrist and fingers that looked like they were always ready to swipe or type.

"My name is Aarav," he said, smiling at the audience as though this were a podcast recording rather than a formal summit. "I work in a fintech start-up. I believe in speed. If something can be done faster, why wait? My biggest frustration? Processes that are designed to slow us down instead of help us move forward. If I can WhatsApp the CEO, why should I wait for three levels of approval?"

A murmur went around the hall—half amused, half scandalized. Aarav sat down confidently, crossing his arms as if daring the managers to roll their eyes.

Next, a young woman stood up. Meera. She was dressed simply, but her voice carried conviction.

"I'm Meera," she said. "I work in a marketing agency, and I care about growth—not just titles, but learning. If I stop learning, I leave. For me, loyalty isn't about how many years I stay. It's about whether the place I'm in is helping me grow. And if it's not, then yes, I'll move on."

I noticed several managers in the audience exchange glances, one even shaking his head. But I also saw a few younger attendees nodding vigorously, as if she had spoken for them.

The third Gen Z rep stood without hesitation. This was Kabir, broad-shouldered, eyes that sparkled with something larger than his corporate role.

"I'm Kabir," he said. "By day I'm in product design, by night I work on my own start-up idea. For me, work is not just about salary, it's about building something that has meaning. I don't want to just follow instructions. I want to create. If that means challenging the way things are, then so be it."

His words had a different weight, more daring, less defensive. A few audience members leaned forward, clearly intrigued.

Finally, the fourth rep, Riya, stood up. Calm, composed, with an easy smile.

"My name is Riya," she said. "I'm an HR associate. I value balance. Work is important, but so is life. If we don't set boundaries, we burn out. If we burn out, no organization benefits. For me, work should fit into life, not the other way around."

Her tone was steady, and for the first time, even some of the older managers seemed to nod in agreement.

I looked at the four of them: Aarav with his impatience, Meera with her hunger for growth, Kabir with his entrepreneurial spark, and Riya with her quiet insistence on balance. Together, they embodied not just a generation, but the range of contradictions within it.

"This," Mrs Nair said to the hall, "is Gen Z. Not one voice, but many. Not one demand, but a spectrum of them. Over the next four days, they'll represent more than themselves; they'll represent a drift that is already reshaping workplaces everywhere."

I turned my gaze to the right, where four more chairs waited. "And now, let's hear from the managers who live in the middle of this storm."

Unlike the Gen Z reps, who looked as if they'd been ready to leap into the debate since the morning, the managers sat with a more measured composure. Shoulders squared, expressions guarded, the kind of calm you learn after years of carrying deadlines on your back and teams on your shoulders.

"Now," Mr. Mehra said, "let's meet the managers, the ones who have to hold the rope from both ends. Introduce yourselves. Tell us what you stand for, and what frustrates you most."

The first to rise was Mr. Desai. His salt-and-pepper hair and neatly pressed shirt gave away decades of corporate discipline. He clasped his hands behind his back and looked at the hall like a teacher addressing a restless class.

"I'm Desai," he began. "I've spent 22 years in operations. For me, loyalty and discipline are the foundation of work. In our time, you didn't question your manager; you learned from them. You didn't switch jobs every year; you built credibility. My frustration? The sense that rules no longer matter, that hierarchy is treated as an inconvenience instead of the backbone of an organization."

The older executives in the audience nodded almost instinctively, as if they had heard their own voices echoed. Aarav smirked and muttered something under his breath; Meera leaned forward, already preparing her counterpoint.

Next was Ms. Sharma. She wore a soft-colored saree, her expression warm but firm. She smiled as she began.

"I'm Sharma, currently leading a regional sales team. My role puts me in the middle, managing expectations from above and energy from below. I believe in results, but I also believe in relationships. My biggest challenge? Balancing the impatience of younger employees with the targets I must meet. I don't dismiss their ideas, but sometimes I wish they understood that not everything can change overnight."

Her words carried a diplomacy that drew a few nods from both sides. Even Riya, the balance-seeker, seemed to soften at her tone.

The third manager rose with a sigh that seemed to come from his very bones. Mr. Kapoor. His tie was slightly loosened, his eyes tired but sharp, the kind of man who had seen enough boardroom storms to know when another was brewing.

"I'm Kapoor. I've worked in manufacturing supply chains for over fifteen years. My truth? I am tired. Tired of firefighting, tired of attrition, tired of explaining to every new recruit why the basics still matter. I respect the energy of Gen Z, but I worry about their focus. Too often, passion seems to run faster than responsibility. And when that happens, it's managers like us who clean up the mess."

There was a ripple of sympathy in the hall. Even a few Gen Z faces softened, recognizing the exhaustion in his voice.

Finally, the fourth manager stood. Ms. Thomas. Tall, confident, with an air of someone used to negotiating difficult rooms.

"I'm Thomas, head of corporate communications. I've always believed leadership is about listening as much as speaking. What I admire about Gen Z is their courage to voice what earlier generations only thought quietly. But my frustration? Sometimes their voice is so loud that they forget that listening is equally important. Debate is healthy. Disruption is not."

Her words landed with a kind of balance, neither defensive nor aggressive. She sat back down, folding her notes neatly on her lap.

I looked at the four of them: Desai with his loyalty to tradition, Sharma with her pragmatism, Kapoor with his fatigue, and Thomas with her measured diplomacy. They represented not just management, but the weight of responsibility that comes with being caught between two forces: expectations from above and demands from below.

"This is mid-level management. The bridge, the buffer, sometimes even the battlefield. And in the coming days, they will debate head-on with our Gen Z representatives, so that perhaps—just perhaps, we can understand where the drift begins, and where it can lead."

I let the silence hang for a moment, watching both sides steal glances at each other, curious, cautious, already sharpening their points.

I looked from left to right—four Gen Z representatives, four managers—like two teams waiting at the starting line. The air was already heavy with anticipation, but I didn't want the first real exchange to explode into conflict just yet.

"Before we dive into structured debates," I said, "let's start with something simple. An ice-breaker. One line, from each of you, about what you think is the biggest workplace challenge between your generation and the other. Nothing more, nothing less."

I turned to the Gen Z side first. Aarav leaned forward immediately, almost too eager, like he had been waiting for this invitation all morning.

"One line?" he asked, grinning. "Okay. Biggest challenge? Managers confuse control with leadership."

A ripple of laughter and gasps spread through the audience. I noticed Desai's jaw tighten, though he kept his expression polite.

Meera spoke next, her tone less sharp but equally pointed. "My biggest challenge? We're told to 'be patient' when what we need are opportunities to grow. Patience without progress isn't a virtue, it's stagnation."

Several young attendees in the audience murmured their agreement. I caught the faintest smile tugging at Riya's lips.

Then Kabir's turn. He didn't hesitate either. "For me, the biggest challenge is this: we bring ideas, but too often, they're dismissed as unrealistic before they're even considered. Innovation dies not because it's wrong, but because it's inconvenient."

There was a pause, heavier this time. I could see Thomas taking mental notes, her eyes sharp, calculating.

Finally, Riya. She was calm, even gentle. "The assumption that long hours equal dedication. They don't. Productivity has to be measured differently. Otherwise, we're just rewarding exhaustion."

There was some applause from the audience at that, even from a few managers who had clearly felt the sting of late nights themselves.

I then turned toward the managers. "Now, your turn. One line each. Keep it sharp."

Desai wasted no time. "My challenge? Gen Z mistakes questioning authority for wisdom. Sometimes rules exist because they work."

The hall reacted with murmurs—half in approval, half in protest. Aarav smirked but said nothing, though I could see the retort burning on his tongue.

Sharma followed, her voice steady but not unkind. "For me, the challenge is balancing ambition with reality. Ambition without patience is just restlessness."

Some heads nodded quietly at that, even among the younger audience members.

Kapoor sighed before speaking, as though the sentence carried the weight of his career. "My challenge? Retention. We invest time and effort in training young employees, but they leave before the ink on their ID cards has dried. It feels like building a bridge while the other side is already moving away."

The metaphor drew a low hum of agreement across the hall. Even Kabir tilted his head slightly, perhaps conceding a point.

And finally, Thomas. "My challenge is not Gen Z's voice, it is their volume. Speaking up is valuable. Shouting over everyone else is not."

Her tone was calm, but the words landed firmly. I noticed Riya shift slightly in her seat, thoughtful rather than defensive.

When the last words faded, I let the silence grow. The tension was palpable; not hostility, not yet, but the kind of sharp edge that promised sparks when real debates began.

"Good," Mr Mehra said finally, breaking the pause. "You've all given us a taste of what's to come. And if this is what you sound like in one line, I can only imagine what four days will hold."

There was laughter, light and uneasy, but it loosened the room just enough.

I straightened my notes. "This afternoon, we begin with our first debate: The Loyalty Question. For now, let's pause, breathe, and prepare. Because when we return, the gloves come off."

The applause that followed was louder, mixed with excitement and just the faintest thread of nerves.

As the applause faded, I closed my notebook and looked out at the hall. The energy had shifted—no longer polite anticipation, but a current of something sharper, more electric. Both sides had revealed their edges, and the audience had tasted the clash to come.

"This," Mrs Nair said slowly, "is exactly why we're here. Eight voices, each carrying the weight of their own truths, and a room full of witnesses who will push us further. I warned you it would get uncomfortable. I think we're already there."

A few chuckles rippled through the crowd. Even Kapoor, the weary manager, allowed himself the faintest smile.

Mrs Nair leaned forward, lowering her voice just slightly. "But remember this is not theatre. These aren't rehearsed lines. What happens here matters because every one of us will walk out of this summit carrying something back to our workplaces. My hope is not that you agree with each other, but that you understand each other."

The words seemed to land differently across the hall; some nodding, some thoughtful, a few skeptics still stiff in their seats. But that was fine. Agreement wasn't the goal.

I tapped the folder in front of me, marked with the first agenda. "When we return after lunch, we begin our first structured debate. We'll start with the question that sparked this entire summit in the first place: Loyalty. What does it mean? Is it time served, or is it value exchanged? Do we measure it in years, or in growth?"

I let the questions linger in the air. Aarav leaned back in his chair, already smirking as though he had his arguments lined up like arrows in a quiver. Desai sat with arms folded, eyes fixed firmly on the stage, his expression unreadable, but his posture telling me he was ready to defend old ground. Between them, the distance was less than ten feet. In meaning, it felt like a canyon.

"Take your break," I said finally. "Eat, breathe, recharge. Because when we come back, the first sparks will fly."

The room broke into a mix of chatter and footsteps, people stretching, heading toward the coffee counters. The Gen Z representatives huddled briefly, laughing and whispering like a team before a big match. Across the aisle, the managers exchanged fewer words, but their silence was just as telling; measured, strategic, preparing to hold their ground.

I stayed seated for a moment, watching them both. The summit had only just begun, but I could already feel the weight of what was ahead. The airport conversation that had started this all seemed like a distant whisper now. The voices in this room were louder, sharper, and far more urgent.

CHAPTER TWO

THE LOYALTY QUESTION

After lunch, the summit hall carried a different kind of energy; lighter in some corners, heavier in others. Morning pleasantries were behind us; now people had settled into their roles. The casual conversations over tea and sandwiches had only sharpened the anticipation for what was next.

I walked back to my seat at the center of the stage, flanked by Mrs. Nair on my left and Mr. Mehra on my right. Together, we exchanged a brief glance; we all knew the session we were about to begin would stir the strongest emotions yet.

The two rows facing us were already in place. On my left, the Gen Z representatives: Aarav tapping his sneakered foot under the table, restless as ever; Meera with her laptop already open, her fingers hovering as if she couldn't resist recording every word; Riya absentmindedly sketching stars in her notebook, her calm masking a quiet sharpness; and Kabir, straight-backed, glasses catching the light, his expression patient but alert.

On the right sat the managers. Mr. Kapoor, his arms folded firmly across his chest, the picture of silent judgment. Mr. Desai, dignified but visibly weary, as though he had carried this conversation many times before. Ms. Sharma, measured and diplomatic, her pen perfectly aligned with her notebook. And Ms. Thomas, quietly scribbling already, her notes shielded like secrets.

The audience was just returning from their lunch break, still murmuring as they settled into rows of seats. A few young professionals leaned forward eagerly, waiting for sparks to fly. Some older leaders leaned back, arms crossed, their expressions suggesting they already knew how this conversation would unfold.

I leaned toward the microphone, letting the quiet build. "We now begin with the issue I've heard most often in corridors, boardrooms, and if I'm honest—even in airport lounges. Loyalty. Or, as many managers call it these days, *the disappearance of it.*"

The room stilled. Mr. Kapoor gave a slow, emphatic nod, as though I had just spoken his own thoughts aloud. Across the table, Meera adjusted her chair, her eyes steady and unflinching.

I continued. "Here is the story I hear time and again: We bring in bright young professionals. We train them. We invest our time, our budgets, our trust. And just when it feels like they're ready to deliver, they're gone. Off to the next job, the next company, the next dream. Colleagues are left scrambling, projects half-finished, and the managers who believed in them feel… abandoned."

I scanned both sides of the stage. "So here's the question before us: *What does loyalty mean?* Is it about the years you spend in a company, or is it about the impact you create while you're there?"

The audience stirred. A few managers muttered in agreement, their heads nodding vigorously. Across the room, some of the younger attendees exchanged glances that said more than words ever could; *finally, the real question has been asked.*

The air tightened, charged, as though everyone in the hall knew we were about to step into dangerous but necessary ground.

This was no longer small talk from a lunch table. It was the heart of a generational divide. And now, it was about to be laid bare.

I took a sip of water and let the room settle. We had named the tension. Now it needed shape. Not a verdict, not yet. First, a few stories that had been following me across terminals and corridors for months.

The first was from an airport, of course. I was in the security line when a plant head from a large auto supplier recognised me and struck up a conversation. He spoke in a low voice, almost like a confession. "We hire graduates, we train them for six months, they learn our machines and our rhythm, then by the ninth month, they have a better offer. I do not even get to see them at their first anniversary." He shook his head, then added something that stayed with me. "I do not feel angry, I feel invisible." That word stayed, invisible. Not unappreciated, not underpaid, invisible. It said more about loyalty than any spreadsheet.

A week later, in a hotel lobby after a client dinner, I met a young product manager who was packing her laptop into a tote bag covered with stickers. She had worked in three companies in five years. I asked why she moved so often. She smiled, not defensive, simply clear. "I move when the learning curve flattens. I do not want to sit in a meeting and feel my mind shut down. If the work stops growing me, I change the work." She listed what each move had given her. First job, technical depth. Second, exposure to scale. Third, context about users. There was no swagger in her voice, only method.

A campus visit gave me another lens. During a placement talk, a student asked me a question that would have sounded outrageous twenty years ago but now felt almost practical. "If I join your company, what will you do in the first twelve months to make me better than I am today?" He did not ask about CTC, not first. He asked about growth. In that moment I realised how differently the two sides open the conversation. Managers often begin with cost and risk. Gen Z often begins with learning and momentum. If the two openings do not meet, we are already negotiating from different maps.

I looked back at the hall. "I want to offer two models," I said. "Not to declare one as right and the other as wrong, but to give us a language."

"The first is the old model of loyalty. Many of us grew up inside it. You joined a company and stayed. Ten years meant you could be trusted with more. Twenty years meant you were part of the furniture, in the best sense. You knew the system, the people, the unwritten rules. Pensions existed. Long service awards meant something because service itself meant something. The organisation was not just a workplace; it was a place of belonging. Loyalty was time."

Mr. Kapoor's shoulders softened a little. Mr. Desai nodded once, as if greeting an old colleague. I understood that feeling. There was dignity in that model. There was also safety. Sometimes safety becomes comfort, and comfort becomes stagnation. We do not need to insult the past to see its limits.

"The second is the new model," I continued. "A portfolio career. Not one ladder but many steps. You build a stack of skills, each role a project that teaches you something different. Your loyalty is to growth and to the value you can create, not to a calendar. You stay while the relationship serves both sides, and when the mutual value thins out, you move. Loyalty is impact."

Across the table, Aarav was already nodding. Meera looked down at her screen and typed a quick line, probably a note she wanted to use later. Riya's pen paused over a small star she was sketching. Kabir listened without expression, which usually meant he was processing every word.

Mrs. Nair leaned toward her mic. "Both models produce pride," she said quietly. "One takes pride in staying. The other takes pride in compounding. We must be careful not to reduce either to a caricature."

I agreed. "There is a reason our parents and mentors wore tenure like a badge. It built trust. It preserved memory. Teams need both. And there is a reason the new generation values movement. Markets change quickly. Technology rewrites the job every few years. If you do not move, you risk becoming a specialist in something the world no longer needs."

I shared one more story, because numbers rarely change minds, but stories sometimes do. A founder told me about a young engineer who left his company after fourteen months. The founder was upset for weeks. Later, a client demo broke. That old engineer, now in a new firm, picked up the phone and helped the team fix it in twenty minutes. No invoice, no drama. The founder told me, "I realised he had not left us. He had left our payroll. There is a difference." It was an uncomfortable sentence, but it opened a door. We speak about loyalty like a cord that snaps. Sometimes it is a thread that stretches.

Mr. Mehra turned slightly toward me. "So what are we asking them to choose?" he said. "Time, or value?"

"Neither," I said. "We are asking them to negotiate value over time. That is different." I paused to let the line land. "If the organisation offers growth, trust, and meaningful work, people stay longer. If the individual brings impact, learning, and reliability, the organisation invests deeper. It is a value exchange. The calendar measures the relationship; it does not define it."

I could see a few heads in the audience tilt, the way people do when a thought moves a click forward. A senior HR leader in the third row wrote something on a card and passed it to a colleague. A young engineer in the fifth row whispered to the person next to him and gestured with his hands as if mapping a graph in the air.

"Here is a simple frame," I said. "Ask two questions, from both sides. One, what is the value created so far? Two, what is the value still possible here? If both answers feel strong, stay and deepen. If the first is strong but the second looks thin, plan a respectful transition. If both are weak, something upstream is broken. Fix the design, not just the mood."

I did not want this to sound like a theory, so I anchored it in practice. For leaders, create visible growth lanes, not just titles. Offer six-month skills sprints with clear outcomes. Make managers teachers, not gatekeepers. Close the loop on trust, give autonomy and then review outcomes without suspicion. For Gen Z, build credibility you can carry. Finish what you start. Make your impact legible, not just real. When you leave, leave bridges, not bruises.

The hall was very quiet now. Not tense, just attentive. We had not solved loyalty in ten minutes, but we had changed its shape. That often helps. People can negotiate shape.

I looked at both rows again. "We will hear your stories next," I said. "But before we do that, I want to say this aloud so we do not forget it once the examples start to pull us to extremes. Loyalty is not a moral medal. It is a living contract. It asks, What do we give each other, and for how long. That is all."

Mrs. Nair added a gentle closing line. "And when we say long, we should learn to count in learning, not only in years."

A light murmur rose from the audience. Some smiles, a few nods, a few folded arms that were a little less tight. I closed my folder and rested my hands on the table.

"All right," I said. "Let us listen to those who live this question every day."

I turned to the left. Aarav was ready.

"I'll start," he said quickly, not waiting for me to invite him by name. His voice carried the restless energy of someone who disliked pauses.

"My first job lasted eighteen months. Everyone said I was impatient. But in those eighteen months, I learned a coding language, helped automate an internal process, and built a dashboard that the company still uses. Eighteen months. Do you know what I would have learned in a second year? The same things I already knew. Why would I sit still just to collect a calendar badge?"

He paused, looking directly at Mr. Kapoor, whose folded arms remained as still as stone.

"Every move I've made has been for learning. New projects, new teams, new challenges. To me, that's loyalty—to my own growth and to the work I deliver while I'm there. If you want me to stay longer, give me something new to chew on."

The audience buzzed. Some younger professionals clapped lightly; the managers exchanged tight glances. I could feel the old wound being poked.

Meera closed her laptop slowly, as though her words needed full presence. Her tone was quieter but sharper, like a scalpel.

"My parents both stayed in the same companies for decades. They were steady, reliable, and hardworking. And yet, almost every night, I watched them come home frustrated. They didn't leave because they were told loyalty meant staying. But loyalty without growth isn't noble, it's suffocating."

She took a breath. "I worked three years in a stable marketing firm. It paid well. The office was comfortable. But after a point, the work stopped challenging me. I knew exactly what each quarter would look like. When I left for a start-up, people called me reckless. But at the start-up, I launched three campaigns in six months, failed twice, succeeded once, and grew more than I had in the three years before. That's loyalty to impact. That's loyalty to myself. If a company wants me to stay, it has to show me I'm still alive inside it."

"I believe we are loyal," Riya said. "But our loyalty is not to permanence, it's to balance, to well-being, to fairness. I stayed in one HR role for two years because my manager invested in me. She cared about my boundaries, and she respected when I needed time. That loyalty went both ways. I stayed longer than I planned, not because of the salary, but because of the respect."

Her eyes swept gently across the audience. "But I've also left. And when I did, I felt guilty. Guilty that people would see me as disloyal. But over time, I realised guilt is misplaced. If staying means burnout, then leaving is not disloyalty, it's survival. And survival is the first duty we all have to ourselves. A company that expects loyalty without protecting well-being is asking for devotion, not commitment."

Mr. Desai nodded slightly, though I wasn't sure if it was agreement or recognition of reality, but it was an unexpected reaction.

Kabir was the last. He pushed his glasses up and spoke slowly, with the precision of someone who thinks before every word.

"I don't switch jobs often," he began. "But when I do, people assume it's because I'm chasing something shinier. That's not true. Every exit I've made has been after finishing something important. I don't leave mid-stream. I leave after the contribution."

He paused, looking toward the managers' table. "When I left my last role, my manager told me I had betrayed the team. That word, betrayal stayed with me. I asked myself, did I betray them? Or did I deliver, grow, and then move on when the relationship had given all it could? I realised I had not broken loyalty. I had fulfilled it. Loyalty doesn't always mean staying forever. Sometimes it means giving fully, leaving bridges intact, and then stepping into the next chapter."

Listening to them, I didn't hear arrogance. I heard clarity. They were reshaping it. For them, loyalty wasn't measured in the weight of a service certificate. It was measured in what they left behind: dashboards, campaigns, balance and bridges.

I leaned into the microphone. "What you've told us is simple but radical. That loyalty is not time but impact."

I shifted my gaze to the other side of the table. The side that had years of experience in holding teams together while people walked out the door. "Now, let's hear from the managers. What does loyalty mean to you, and what does it feel like when it disappears?"

Mr. Kapoor was the first to lean into his microphone. His voice carried the kind of fatigue that doesn't need dramatics to be real. "I've worked in supply chains for fifteen years. Factories don't forgive inconsistency. When a young engineer leaves after six months, it isn't just a line item in HR; it's production delays, missed deadlines, and broken client trust. I've had to stand in front of customers and explain why a deliverable was late, not because our machines failed, but because our people left."

He exhaled slowly. "I am not against growth. But what I struggle with is this: every exit means weeks of backfilling, retraining, and handholding. Every exit means the ones who stay carry double the load. So when someone tells me they gave their 'best' for a year and then moved on, I don't see loyalty. I see a half-built bridge left for me to finish."

There was no anger in his tone—only exhaustion. And somehow, that weighed more heavily on the room than anger ever could.

Mr. Desai adjusted his glasses, his posture upright, his presence calm but firm. "I've been in operations for over two decades. I come from a time when credibility was earned by staying, by proving consistency over years, not months. That consistency gave managers the confidence to trust you with bigger responsibilities. Today, when a résumé has five jobs in six years, I don't see versatility. I see someone who never stayed long enough to be accountable for the consequences of their work."

He glanced briefly at Aarav, then continued. "I once mentored a young professional who was bright, no doubt about it. He left just as he was about to lead his first major project. He said he wanted 'new challenges.' The irony? That project would have given him the challenge he was craving. But he didn't stay long enough to know. That's what frustrates me: loyalty used to mean patience. Now it seems to mean impatience dressed up as ambition."

Ms. Sharma leaned in next. Her voice was softer, but it carried an authority that only comes from balancing targets and people for years. "My challenge isn't just attrition; it's the ripple effect of attrition. When a young associate leaves, clients ask questions. Teams feel abandoned. Morale dips. And the rest of us are forced to stretch ourselves thin until someone new arrives, and by the time they settle, another person leaves. It becomes a revolving door."

She sighed, then smiled faintly. "I don't dismiss Gen Z's hunger. I even admire it. But loyalty has to mean more than *what I got out of this place. It has to mean what I gave consistently over time.* When people stay through both good quarters and bad ones, that's when trust is built. Otherwise, it feels like we are running a never-ending relay where the baton keeps dropping halfway."

Some of the audience nodded at her metaphor. Even Riya, who had spoken about balance earlier, seemed thoughtful.

Finally, Ms. Thomas spoke. Her tone was even, composed, as though she were presenting to a boardroom. "For me, loyalty is not just a number of years; it's about the credibility that builds only with time. You can't replace lived history. You can't substitute the memory of how a crisis was handled five years ago or how a relationship with a client evolved. When people leave too quickly, organisations lose not just skills, but memory. And memory is what gives companies resilience."

She paused, looking at the younger side of the table. "I admire Gen Z's courage to voice what they want. But too often, that voice is so focused on me, my growth, my impact, my purpose—that it forgets the we. Teams don't grow on individual bursts alone. They grow on consistency, on showing up day after day. That, to me, is the true test of loyalty."

Her words were not harsh, but they carried weight. The audience responded with a low murmur, some nodding in agreement, others looking conflicted.

As I listened to the managers, I realised the emotional undertone was not anger. It was something deeper: abandonment. Each of them carried stories of being left behind to hold things together. For them, loyalty wasn't just about staying. It was about staying *long enough*—long enough to finish the bridge, long enough to carry the team through a storm, long enough to build the credibility that only time can gift.

I could see it now: the room wasn't split by age. It was split by experience. On one side, the urgency of growth. On the other hand, the ache of being left to clean up after it.

And as I glanced at the audience, I knew their voices would complicate this picture even further.

I turned towards the rows of faces in front of us. "We've heard the perspectives from both sides of the stage," I said. "Now, let's hear from you, the audience. After all, loyalty isn't a theory. It's something you live every day in your teams and careers. Who would like to share?"

A hand shot up from the second row. The man stood, mid-forties, salt-and-pepper hair, still carrying the posture of someone who had worn the same ID badge for a long time.

"I've spent twenty years in the same company," he began. "When I joined, I was proud of the idea of retiring from the same organisation. I believed loyalty was about staying the course, no matter what. But now, when I look back, I wonder if I confused loyalty with fear of change. Yes, I was rewarded with stability. Yes, I climbed the ladder. But I also missed opportunities because I didn't move. Sometimes I think I stayed loyal to the wrong thing, that is, security, when I should have been loyal to my own growth."

A hush settled over the room. It was unusual to hear someone challenge their own choices so openly. Aarav looked almost vindicated. Mr. Desai, however, gave a small nod, acknowledging the courage it took to say that aloud.

Next, a younger voice—perhaps early thirties— rose from the back. She introduced herself as an HR manager at a multinational.

"In my experience, job mobility isn't disloyalty; it's reality," she said. "We can't expect employees to commit for ten years when industries reinvent themselves every three. In fact, I often encourage young hires to switch roles internally every twelve to eighteen months. It keeps them engaged, prevents stagnation, and builds breadth. If we don't create those pathways inside, they'll find them outside. That doesn't make them disloyal. It makes them ambitious."

Another hand rose, a man in his late thirties, voice tinged with weariness. "I lead a customer support team. In the last year, I've lost six people. Each time, I had to cover their shifts until replacements came in. I don't begrudge them for moving. But let me be honest, it feels like abandonment. We say loyalty is about value exchange, but when you leave suddenly, who holds the burden? Us. The ones who stay. So forgive me if I sound bitter, but when attrition hits, it's not an abstract concept; it's extra hours, extra calls, extra weight. For me, loyalty means staying long enough not to leave others drowning."

This drew murmurs of agreement from several managers in the hall. Even Kabir, usually impassive, tapped his pen softly, as though acknowledging the truth of the burden.

A woman in her late twenties stood next. Her blazer sleeves were rolled up, her energy quick, kinetic. "I run a five-year-old start-up. My average employee tenure? Thirteen months. At first, I fought it. I begged people to stay. But then I realised: they left behind products, features, ideas that still live in our company. One designer left us for a big tech firm, but her wireframes are still the backbone of our app. Another engineer left, but the automation he built still saves us hours every week. I've learned to see loyalty differently; it's not about forever. It's about leaving something behind that lasts longer than your notice period." Her words caught both sides off guard.

I leaned forward, my voice softer now.

"What we've just heard proves something important. Loyalty isn't one thing. For some, it is stability. For others, it is growth. For some, it is patience. For others, it is a legacy. And for many, it is all of those at different points in their careers."

The hall was still, listening. "Maybe the mistake we make is treating loyalty like a universal constant. But in reality, it's contextual. It changes with age, with roles, with seasons of life. It is loyalty to the company, yes, but also to growth, to the team, to survival. The problem isn't that one side is wrong. The problem is that we're using the same word to mean very different things."

Mrs Nair, Mr Mehra, and I leaned back in our seats, soaking in the discussion. We did not want to come to a conclusion; we wanted to draw an analysis and bring up a solution that favoured both parties.

"Here's what I'm hearing from all of you—whether you're a Gen Z professional, a manager, or someone in the audience. Loyalty isn't dead. It's just speaking two different languages."

I held up two fingers. "One: For managers, loyalty means time. You stayed through the storm. You built credibility through consistency. You didn't leave when things got hard. That kind of loyalty was visible, tangible, and you could point to the years and say: this is proof."

I raised two more fingers. "Two: For Gen Z, loyalty means impact. Did I contribute? Did I grow? Did I leave behind something useful? If yes, then my loyalty has been fulfilled, even if I was here for only eighteen months."

The hall was quiet. Both definitions had been voiced before, but hearing them side by side, distilled like this, made the clash obvious.

"So which one is right?" I asked. "Neither. And both."

A few people smiled faintly at the paradox.

I continued, "Loyalty today is not a moral medal pinned to your chest. It's a contract. A living, breathing contract. It asks: *What do I give you, and what do you give me, and for how long does that exchange make sense?"*

I could see pens moving quickly across notebooks now. Some heads nodded, others tilted, thinking.

"To explain it simply, let me borrow from another space. Think about brand loyalty. Ten years ago, if you bought the same detergent every month, you were a loyal customer. Today? Loyalty looks different. You might try a new eco-friendly brand, switch to a subscription, or use two products depending on context. Are you disloyal? No. You're making choices based on value, convenience, and alignment with your needs. The brand earns your loyalty continuously, not permanently."

I paused, watching the audience digest the analogy.

"Workplace loyalty is moving the same way. It's not a single marriage to one company forever. It's a series of relationships; some short, some long—defined by the value both sides bring. If the company invests in me, challenges me, respects me, I stay. If I contribute impact, deliver outcomes, and respect the team, I'm loyal. The day that value exchange thins out on either side, the contract ends. Not because someone betrayed the other, but because the relationship served its purpose."

Mrs. Nair leaned toward her mic, adding softly, "And when it ends respectfully, it doesn't have to feel like abandonment. It can feel like a graduation."

I nodded. "Exactly. The problem is not that people leave. The problem is how we leave, and what we leave behind. If you finish what you started, if you leave bridges instead of bruises, that is loyalty. If organisations create growth paths and trust, people will stay longer. If not, they'll go, but even then, their contributions can outlive their tenure."

I glanced around the hall. "So maybe the real question isn't *Is loyalty about years or about impact?* The real question is: *How do we design workplaces where loyalty in both forms, time and impact, can coexist? Because that's the only way forward."*

I closed my notebook and looked across the hall. The stories we'd heard of dashboards built in eighteen months, of managers holding unfinished bridges, of veterans questioning their own choices, were proof enough. Loyalty wasn't gone. It had simply evolved.

But conversations like this mean little unless we walk away with practices we can carry back into our workplaces. So I decided to draw the threads together into two simple lists: one for leaders, one for Gen Z.

For Leaders

- **Redefine loyalty as engagement.** Don't measure only by tenure; measure by the impact and energy people bring while they're with you.

- **Build growth pathways.** If you don't give them new challenges, they'll go elsewhere to find them.
- **Close the trust loop.** Give autonomy, but also follow up with fair outcomes and recognition.
- **Respect exits.** If someone leaves after contributing, treat it as part of the relationship cycle, not a betrayal.

For Gen Z

- **Balance ambition with credibility.** Growth is important, but consistency builds trust. Don't leave before your contribution is visible.
- **Finish what you start.** Deliver outcomes that can outlast your tenure—leave bridges, not gaps.
- **Learn patience alongside passion.** The challenge you're seeking might be just around the corner if you stay long enough to see it.
- **Respect the "we."** Loyalty isn't just to growth; it's also to the team that depends on you.

I leaned into the microphone and said simply, "Thank you for your honesty. We've redefined loyalty. But tomorrow, we ask the next question: What do we do with hierarchy?"

CHAPTER THREE

THE HIERARCHY STRUGGLE

The second morning of the summit began with sharper edges. Conversations in the lobby buzzed louder, with yesterday's debate on loyalty still spilling over into coffee breaks.

Some managers huddled in quiet groups, shaking their heads and whispering. Meanwhile, the young delegates laughed more freely. It was clear that the generational lines had not blurred overnight.

In a few minutes, the auditorium started filling again with the buzzing energy from the delegates. I took my seat at the center of the stage, Mrs. Nair to my left, Mr. Mehra to my right. Across from us, the Gen Z panel was already restless: Aarav leaned back with a grin that dared someone to challenge him; Meera's laptop was open, her fingers poised; Riya sat with her usual calm, though the way she tapped her pen hinted at anticipation; Kabir sat quietly, but his eyes never stopped scanning the hall.

On the managers' side, I noticed a subtle difference. Mr. Kapoor's arms were folded tighter than yesterday. Mr. Desai's eyes were sharper, no longer weary but watchful. Ms. Sharma, still poised, looked determined to cut through the noise with balance. And Ms. Thomas had her notes neatly stacked, as if ready for battle.

I tapped the microphone. "Yesterday, we asked whether loyalty was about years or about impact. We learned that the word has two very different meanings, depending on where you sit. Today, we touch something even more sensitive."

"Hierarchy."

A ripple moved through the hall. Some smiled knowingly. Others shifted in their seats, bracing themselves.

I continued, "Every workplace has invisible lines. Designations. Titles. Approvals. For some, these are the backbone of discipline. For others, they are shackles that block innovation. And so the question we ask this morning is this: *Should respect come from designation, or should it be earned?"*

I could already see reactions forming. Aarav leaned forward, his sneaker tapping fast against the floor. Mr. Kapoor shook his head almost imperceptibly. Somewhere in the audience, a younger voice muttered, "Finally."

I spread my hands across the desk. "This is not an abstract question. It lives in every skipped chain of command, every email sent directly to the CEO, every meeting where a junior interrupts a senior, every Slack message that bypasses three levels. Respect and hierarchy are they tied together, or should they stand apart?"

The room was silent, but not calm. It was the silence of sharpened edges, of people holding their breaths before the first clash.

I looked from left to right. Eight faces, two generations, and one question that would test not just patience but the very structure of the workplace.

"The Loyalty Question tested our commitment," I said slowly. "But the Hierarchy Struggle will test our authority. Now, before we hear your stories, I want to give us a frame. Not a verdict, just a map."

I started where so many of my realizations begin—at an airport. A COO I know met him near Gate 14 and told me about a Monday town hall where a junior analyst asked him, live on video, why the company still required manager approval for basic software tools. She didn't route it through her lead. She didn't soften the question. She asked directly, and thousands watched. He felt blindsided, even disrespected. "What happened to the chain of command?" he asked me. Then he added, softer, "But she was right." They changed the policy in a week.

A week later, at a vendor review, a plant supervisor complained about "Slack sovereignty." His phrase, not mine. "Everyone DMs everyone," he said. "No lanes. A junior pings procurement, legal, the CFO, sometimes all at once." In his world, machines, safety, compliance—skipping steps isn't a style issue; it's a risk. He wasn't defending ego. He was defending order.

I looked across the stage. "This is the heart of it. In one context, bypassing level surfaces truth. In another, it breaks discipline."

I drew two columns on the notepad in front of me, more for my own clarity than the audience's.

Old Model (Hierarchy = Discipline).

This is the world many of us grew up in. Designations signal scope. Decisions move upward, execution moves downward. Respect is given first, earned later. You learn the system before you change it. Authority protects the mission; deadlines, safety, compliance, brand risk.

The promise: predictability. The price: slowness and sometimes silence.

New Model (Flat = Openness).

This is the world our younger colleagues inhabit. Digital flattens distance. If you can tag the CEO in a channel, why wait three layers? Information is horizontal, not just vertical. Respect is earned first, not assumed. You test ideas in public, iterate in daylight. The promise: speed and truth. The price: noise and sometimes chaos.

Mrs. Nair leaned toward her mic. “Both models fail in their extremes,” she said. “Pure hierarchy suffocates initiative; pure flatness erodes accountability.”

Mr. Mehra nodded. “What we’re really asking,” he added, “is not ‘hierarchy or flat,’ but ‘how much of each, where, and when?’”

I turned back to the audience. “Two more stories, because the edges are where the lessons live.”

In a consumer-tech company, a young designer bypassed her manager and shared a prototype directly in the executive channel. The idea flew. Users loved it in testing. Revenue followed. Her skip-level share, by the book, was “wrong.” By the outcome, it was essential. The VP later told me, “If she’d waited for approvals, the moment would’ve passed.”

In a healthcare firm, a junior escalated a sensitive client issue in a public forum, triggering panic. Legal had context the junior didn’t. The client saw screenshots. A fixable issue became a reputational incident. The manager's post-mortem was blunt: "Hierarchy exists so the right people hold the right risk."

I looked at both panels. "So what do we do with that?"

Here's the language I use with my own teams: **There are two kinds of power in organisations: role power and trust power.** Role power comes from designation; it's the right to decide. Trust power comes from credibility; it's the right to be heard. Healthy cultures let trust power travel fast while role power remains clear.

I turned a page. "There's also a timing problem hiding here. Early-career professionals often think respect is earned purely by freshness: new eyes, new tools, new speed. Mid-career managers think respect is earned by weathering storms: deadlines met, crises handled, teams held together. Both are right. Respect has two fuels: freshness and history. Hierarchy over-indexed on history for years; digital over-indexes on freshness today. We need both."

I paused and let the room exhale. "If yesterday was about redefining loyalty as value exchange, then today is about redefining respect as accountable openness. Open voice, accountable role."

A final image, to make it practical. "Think of your organisation like an operating theatre. The surgeon leads (role power). But anybody, be it a nurse, a tech, or an intern, can call out a safety risk on the spot (trust power). The incision doesn't wait for a three-step approval, and nobody shames the person who speaks up. Yet, the intern doesn't decide the surgical plan at the table because they feel strongly. Voice is open; decision is clear."

I let the analogy settle. A few people in the front row were already typing it verbatim.

"So here's the map for the rest of our conversation," I said, tapping the desk lightly.

- **Where the stakes are low and learning is high** (design sprints, ideation, internal tools), flatten aggressively. Let ideas skip levels; speed beats protocol.
- **Where the stakes are high and risk is real** (safety, legal, client crises, brand), keep the chain tight and the circle small; protocol beats speed.
- **Everywhere in between,** teach skip-levels as a craft, not a rebellion: inform your manager, add context, propose a next step, and own follow-through.

Mr. Mehra summed it up with a line that made a few heads lift. "Respect is not the absence of hierarchy. It's the presence of clarity."

I nodded. "And clarity is what we'll test now, through your stories." I turned to the left, where Aarav was already sitting forward, and then to the right, where Mr. Kapoor's arms had, finally, unfolded.

"Let's hear from the younger delegates first." Mr Mehra announced.

Everybody's eyes were on the left side of the stage, looking at the four youngsters.

"Hierarchy slows us down," Aarav said without hesitation. "Last year, I was working on a fintech product. We found a bug that could've affected thousands of transactions. I had the fix ready in a day, but my manager wanted it reviewed through three separate leads. By the time the approvals came back, the client had already flagged it."

His voice grew sharper. "I don't want to disrespect managers. But respect doesn't come from the title next to your name. It comes from how fast you help me solve a problem. If you block me, don't expect me to bow to your designation. Respect has to be earned, not demanded."

Meera's tone was less fiery than Aarav's, but no less forceful. "In my agency job, hierarchy meant silence. If you wanted to present an idea, it had to pass through your reporting manager, then the senior manager, and then maybe the VP. By the time it reached the client, it was no longer *your* idea, it was a diluted version carrying someone else's voice. After a while, I stopped sharing altogether. Why bother, if my voice didn't count?"

She looked straight at the managers' table. "Hierarchy isn't always discipline. Sometimes, it's erasure. And the sad part? Many of us leave not because we hate the company, but because we can't see ourselves in the work. We're invisible. And when you're invisible, you don't stay."

"I don't hate hierarchy," Riya began, her voice calm and measured. "Structure helps. It gives clarity. But what frustrates me is when hierarchy is treated like a wall instead of a ladder. Once, I escalated a concern about burnout policies. My manager told me it wasn't my place. That I was too junior to understand the bigger picture. Maybe he was right about the bigger picture, but the exhaustion was real. My experience didn't need a title to be valid."

She smiled faintly, not bitterly, just honestly. "I think many of us want hierarchy to be flexible. We're okay with titles. We're okay with roles. But we also want the freedom to be heard, even if we don't have seniority. Respect should flow in both directions. Not just down."

That line, *'respect should flow in both directions,'* was quickly scribbled down by half the audience.

Finally, Kabir leaned forward. His voice was quieter, but it carried the kind of gravity that made people lean in to listen. "In my last role, I had an idea for redesigning part of our product. I asked my manager if I could share it directly with the leadership team. He said no, it wasn't the right time. So I waited. Three months later, leadership announced the exact same idea brought in by an external consultant. I don't blame my manager. He was following the rules. But rules cost us innovation."

He paused, adjusting his glasses. "I'm not against hierarchy. But if it prevents ideas from traveling upward, then it's not protecting the company. It's suffocating it. A good leader doesn't fear being bypassed. A good leader amplifies their people's voices. That's the kind of hierarchy I can respect."

"From where you sit, hierarchy isn't discipline, it's distance. And distance makes you invisible. You're not asking for anarchy. You're asking for access. For respect that is earned, not assumed." I said.

I turned to the managers' side of the table. "But for those who've carried teams through chaos, this sounds less like access and more like defiance. And their stories remind us why hierarchy still matters."

Mr. Kapoor was the first to speak. His voice was flat, steady, and almost weary. "In manufacturing, hierarchy is not ego. It's survival. Machines don't forgive mistakes. If a junior skips a safety check because they want to be fast, someone can get hurt. If an engineer bypasses me to approve a change, we could have a system failure. I'm not asking for respect because I'm older. I'm asking for respect because mistakes roll uphill, and managers are the ones held accountable when things break."

He folded his arms again. "You call it 'control.' I call it discipline. Without it, factories don't run, clients don't trust us, and teams collapse. Respect tied to designation is not blind respect. It's respect for responsibility."

The audience stirred, several managers nodding, younger employees frowning.

Mr Desai, with a firm voice said, "I've been in operations for twenty-two years. I know what it takes to keep a system running. I once had a young associate bypass me and email the client directly about a delivery delay. He thought he was being proactive. But he didn't know the context—that we had already negotiated a new timeline with the client. His email undid weeks of careful work. I had to spend days rebuilding that trust."

He glanced briefly at Meera. "I don't oppose fresh ideas. But hierarchy exists because information is layered. A title doesn't just mean authority, it means access to context. Without that, juniors act on half-truths and create bigger problems. So yes, respect should be earned. But so should voice. And earning it means staying long enough to see the whole picture, not just the corner you sit in."

Ms. Sharma adjusted her saree, her tone warmer but no less clear. "Every week, I'm balancing pressure from senior management and energy from younger colleagues. My frustration is not that Gen Z want to speak up, it's that they often want to skip the line without understanding what the line is for."

She paused, softening slightly. "Hierarchy is like traffic lights. You don't always like waiting, but the lights prevent chaos. I once had a junior executive interrupt a client meeting to pitch his own idea. He was creative, no doubt, but he hadn't thought through the financials. The client smiled politely, but later asked me if our team was coordinated. That one interruption cost us credibility. Innovation is valuable, but timing and context matter. That's what hierarchy protects."

Finally, Ms. Thomas, in a calm, deliberate, and almost surgical tone said, "In communications, words matter. Sequence matters. Once, during a crisis, a young associate tweeted from the company account without clearance. His intentions were good; he wanted transparency. But he revealed information that legal hadn't cleared yet. Within minutes, the tweet went viral, and we had a media firestorm. It took weeks to repair the damage. That's why hierarchy exists—not to silence, but to safeguard."

She let the silence linger. "I respect Gen Z's courage to voice ideas. But courage without filters can turn into recklessness. Respecting hierarchy doesn't mean suppressing your voice. It means recognising that leadership carries not just privileges, but liabilities."

"From where you sit, hierarchy is not a wall. It's a safety rail. It doesn't exist to silence, but to prevent collapse. You don't dismiss voice, you just ask that voice to travel with context, with timing, with responsibility." I glanced back at the Gen Z panel. "And here is our tension. To you, hierarchy feels like distance. To them, it feels like discipline. And between distance and discipline, the same structure is seen as either a prison or a backbone."

I turned towards the audience. "We've heard from both panels," I said. "Now let's hear from you; the people who live with hierarchy every day. How does it serve you, and how does it fail you?"

Hands shot up across the hall. I pointed to a man in the third row, who stood with the kind of posture that revealed decades of corporate conditioning.

"I've been in the same company for eighteen years," he began. "And I'll tell you this: hierarchy saved my career more than once. During a product recall, my manager shielded me from direct client anger. He took the heat. If I had faced it alone, my confidence would have shattered. Titles matter because they carry the shield of accountability. Without them, juniors get crushed."

The managers nodded instinctively, relief crossing Mr. Desai's face as though someone else had carried his point forward.

But before the applause faded, another hand shot up.

Next was a young analyst. She couldn't have been more than twenty-five. "I agree hierarchy protects sometimes," she said. "But too often, it silences. I once spotted an error in financial data that could have saved us a major penalty. I told my manager. He said it wasn't my place to raise it higher. Two months later, the error blew up. We paid the penalty. And my idea? Buried under process. That day, I decided: if speaking up means breaking hierarchy, I'll break it."

The audience reacted audibly this time; some clapped, some shook their heads. Aarav gave her a quick thumbs-up. Mr. Kapoor muttered something under his breath, clearly unconvinced.

A man in his late twenties stood next, blazer sleeves rolled up. "In my start-up, we don't have hierarchy. Anyone can pitch directly to me. But let me be honest, it's chaos. Every idea, every complaint, every request lands in my inbox. We move fast, yes, but we burn out. I've realised structure isn't the enemy; bad structure is. What we need is hierarchy as a filter, not a wall."

That line, *'a filter, not a wall,'* was quickly typed into dozens of phones and laptops.

From the middle rows, a woman in her forties raised her hand. "I've spent my career in HR, and I've seen both extremes. In one company, hierarchy was so rigid that innovation died on arrival. In another, hierarchy was so flat that no one knew who was accountable when things went wrong. The truth is simple: hierarchy must breathe. It has to flex. If it becomes too rigid, it breaks people. If it's too loose, it breaks trust."

Her balanced tone earned nods from both sides of the stage. Even Meera, who usually bristled at hierarchy, scribbled something in her notes.

Finally, a nervous voice rose from the back row. "I'm new to consulting. In my first client meeting, I asked a question directly to the CFO. Afterwards, my manager told me I'd overstepped. I felt embarrassed. But the CFO later emailed me to thank me for the question—it was something nobody had raised. So who was right? My manager, who wanted discipline? Or the CFO, who wanted openness? I still don't know."

That uncertainty hung in the air longer than any applause. It revealed what everyone in the room already suspected: hierarchy isn't a question of right or wrong. It's situational.

"Hierarchy is both a shield and a shackle. It protects, but it also silences. It creates order, but sometimes kills ideas. It gives clarity but can erase voices. And the truth is, we don't want to abolish it; we want to design it better." I said. "The challenge is not 'hierarchy or flat.' The challenge is: how do we decide when to use each? How do we create lanes, not walls? How do we protect accountability without killing access?"

I closed my folder and looked across the hall. We had circled the issue from every angle: speed versus stability, openness versus order, voice versus discipline. The lesson was clear: hierarchy is not disappearing, but neither is it absolute. What matters is how we design it.

Mrs Nair, Mr Mehra, and I came up with a few suggestions for both the leaders as well as the Gen Z.

For Leaders

- **Flatten lanes, not accountability.** Create channels where juniors can share ideas directly, but keep decision rights clear.
- **Earn respect daily.** Don't rely on your title. Show competence, fairness, and courage in moments that matter.
- **Teach context.** Before dismissing a young voice as naïve, explain the unseen risks. Context turns rebellion into responsibility.
- **Protect without suffocating.** Be a shield in crises, but also a platform that lifts voices upward.

For Gen Z

- **Use the lanes responsibly.** If you bypass hierarchy, inform your manager and carry the full context.
- **Respect the shield.** Hierarchy often absorbs risks you don't see. Don't mistake silence for irrelevance.
- **Balance courage with timing.** An idea matters, but so does when and how you share it.
- **Remember the "we."** Speaking up is valuable. Listening and aligning afterwards is equally important.

"Hierarchy is no longer just titles; they are about clarity as to what we give and how we listen." I let the pause stretch. "But when you flatten structures and open voices, something else happens. A new hunger rises. If titles can't be the only measure of respect, then people look for recognition elsewhere. And what they ask for—louder, faster, more often—is feedback."

"Let's take a break and be back after lunch for the next session." Mr Mehra announced.

CHAPTER FOUR

THE FEEDBACK FRENZY

Day 2 afternoon carried a very different charge. The morning had been all about authority: who holds it, who challenges it, and what respect really means.

I overheard a younger delegate telling her friend, "Titles don't matter as much as feedback. I just want to know if I'm doing it right, now, not at the end of the year."

Across the hall, a manager sighed to a colleague, "If I give them feedback every day, when will I actually get my own work done?"

It was clear: the next fracture line was waiting.

When the lights dimmed again and the hall settled, I took my seat at the center desk. Mrs. Nair adjusted her glasses beside me, calm as ever. Mr. Mehra leaned forward, scanning the crowd as though he could already sense the sparks about to fly.

On the left the Gen Z were ready with their piece of arguments whereas on the right the managers were ready with their defences.

I leaned into the microphone. "Yesterday, we redefined loyalty. This morning, we reframed hierarchy. And now, we arrive at something more personal, something that sits at the heart of every workplace interaction. Feedback."

I paused, letting the word hang.

"For some, feedback is fuel. It's oxygen. Without it, they feel invisible, uncertain, lost. For others, feedback that is given too often feels like micromanagement, like someone breathing down their neck every hour. So the question we ask this afternoon is this: How much feedback is enough? And when does recognition cross the line into control?"

I looked across the stage. Aarav was already leaning forward, ready to argue that feedback should be as instant as a like on Instagram. Mr. Kapoor shook his head slightly, his expression saying more than words: this is going to be painful.

The room buzzed with anticipation. The debate over hierarchy had been about systems. This one would be about emotions. About validation, insecurity, trust, and control.

I spread my hands on the desk. "Let's talk about the Feedback Frenzy."

"Let me give you two pictures," I began. "One old, one new."

"When I started my career, feedback came once a year. The annual appraisal. You sat across from your manager in a stuffy conference room, sometimes with HR in the corner, and waited to hear if your year had been 'meets expectations' or, if you were lucky, 'exceeds expectations.' That conversation often determined your raise, your promotion, and your morale for the next twelve months. For many of us, it was the most important meeting of the year, and the least useful."

I smiled faintly, because I could see older heads in the audience nodding. "Why the least useful? Because by the time feedback arrived, it was stale. You couldn't correct a mistake from nine months ago. You couldn't celebrate a contribution that had already faded into memory. And yet, this was the system. Structured. Predictable. Infrequent."

Mr. Desai nodded firmly, as though defending the predictability even as I critiqued it.

"Now contrast that with the world many of you live in today. Social media, gaming, apps—all built around instant responses. Post a photo? You know within minutes how people react. Finish a level in a game? You get points immediately. Gen Z grew up in an environment where feedback is not annual, not quarterly, not even weekly; it's continuous."

I gestured toward the Gen Z panel. Riya smiled softly. "In this new model, feedback is expected in real-time. Finish a task? You want to know today if it worked. Share an idea? You want validation or correction—now, not three months later. Feedback isn't seen as micromanagement. It's seen as recognition. Silence feels like absence. For this generation, no news isn't good news, it's neglect."

The younger audience members nodded vigorously. A few even clapped.

"And here lies the struggle," I continued. "For managers, too much feedback feels impossible. 'If I have to comment on every little thing,' one manager told me in an airport lounge, 'when will I do my own job?' For Gen Z, too little feedback feels like rejection. As one young professional told me, 'If my manager doesn't say anything, I assume I failed.'"

I let the contrast hang for a moment.

"So once again, we're not asking whether feedback matters. We're asking how much, how often, and in what form. Is feedback the quarterly sit-down? The daily check-in? The casual Slack emoji? Or all of the above?"

Mrs. Nair leaned toward her mic. "And perhaps more importantly," she added, "how do we give feedback without turning managers into babysitters, and without leaving employees feeling abandoned?"

Mr. Mehra nodded. "That's the needle we'll try to thread."

I looked at both panels. "We know the maps now. One side grew up with annual reviews. The other grew up with instant likes. The question before us: can we build a culture of feedback that fuels performance without becoming noise?"

The room quieted again, ready for the stories. I turned to the Gen Z panel.

"Go ahead," I said. "Tell us why feedback matters the way it does to you."

Aarav jumped in before I had even finished the sentence. "Feedback is fuel," he said, almost too quickly. "It's like oxygen. Without it, I start to doubt myself."

He leaned forward, his voice carrying an edge. "My first job, I worked on a feature update for a fintech app. I stayed late nights, pulled weekends, made sure everything was perfect. When we launched, nobody said a word. No thank you, no review, no comment. Silence. For weeks, I thought I'd failed. Later, I found out the feature was performing well. But by then, the silence had already killed my motivation."

He shrugged. "You can call it fragile if you want. But here's the truth: silence is louder than criticism. I'd rather you tell me it's bad so I can fix it than say nothing at all."

"I once worked in a marketing agency where feedback came only at the end of a campaign. If the results were good, you got a bonus. If they weren't, you got a warning. That was it. No mid-course corrections, no discussions while the work was in progress. Just judgment at the finish line."

Meera's tone sharpened. "Do you know how powerless it feels to spend weeks on something without knowing if you're on the right track? It's like running a marathon blindfolded. By the time you hear the feedback, it's too late to change anything."

She tapped her fingers on the table, then added softly, "When I finally moved to a start-up, I got used to instant feedback. Slack pings, emoji reactions, one-line comments in Google Docs. And it didn't feel like micromanagement. It felt like someone cared enough to pay attention."

Her words landed. Even some of the managers, who had bristled at Aarav's bluntness, leaned in.

Riya stepped in next. "For me, feedback is less about performance and more about connection. I once had a manager who checked in every Friday, not just about tasks, but about how I was doing. Those fifteen minutes made me feel seen. I stayed longer in that job than I ever planned, not because of the salary, but because of that sense of recognition."

She smiled faintly, then added, "Feedback doesn't always have to be formal. Sometimes it's a small gesture; a thank you, a quick message, even an acknowledgment in a meeting. Those little moments keep us going. Without them, work feels transactional. With them, it feels human."

There was a pause in the hall, softer than before. Even Mr. Kapoor, who had looked irritated earlier, nodded slightly at her point.

Kabir adjusted his glasses and spoke in his steady, thoughtful tone. "I see feedback as a map. Without it, you don't know if you're headed north or south. With it, you can course-correct before you're lost."

He paused, choosing his words carefully. "In one role, I worked for months on redesigning part of a product. My manager gave me no input during the process. At the end, he tore it apart in a review meeting in front of the entire team. I felt humiliated. Not because he criticised my work, but because the criticism came too late. If he had given me directions earlier, I could have built something better. Instead, it felt like he was waiting to catch me out."

His voice grew softer. "That's when I realised feedback isn't just about recognition. It's about fairness. If you wait until the end to judge me, you're not helping me grow, you're just keeping score."

As I listened to them, a pattern emerged. Aarav craved immediacy, Meera demanded mid-course corrections,

Riya valued recognition, Kabir sought fairness. Four voices, four shades of the same truth: feedback is not decoration. It is a direction.

I leaned into the microphone. "What you've shown us is that feedback isn't just about performance, it's about belonging, clarity, and growth. To you, silence isn't neutral. It feels like an absence. Recognition, even small, is proof that your work matters."

I turned toward the managers' side. "But for those who carry heavy teams, this hunger can feel overwhelming. And now, we'll hear what feedback looks like from the other side."

Mr. Kapoor spoke first, his tone clipped, his expression tired. "I manage operations in manufacturing. My day is packed with client calls, vendor negotiations, audits, and fire drills. And yet, my team expects me to constantly validate them. *'How was my presentation?' 'Did I handle that call well?' 'Can you give me feedback on this email?'*"

He rubbed his temple. "I'm not dismissing their effort. But when I spend more time commenting than doing, I feel like a babysitter, not a manager. Feedback is important, yes. But it has to be balanced. Otherwise, it becomes micromanagement; not because I want control, but because I can't breathe under the weight of constant requests."

The managers in the audience nodded vigorously. Aarav muttered something under his breath that made Riya nudge him sharply.

"I've seen feedback work both ways. Too little, and people feel lost. Too much, and they stop thinking for themselves. One of my team members once came to me after every client call asking, 'How did I do?' At first, I answered patiently. But over time, I realised he was outsourcing his confidence to me. Instead of developing his own judgment, he was addicted to my approval. That's not feedback, that's dependency." Mr. Desai leaned forward.

"Managers are supposed to build capability, not co-dependency. If I give you a direction at every step, when do you learn to trust your own instincts? Feedback should guide, not babysit. If it becomes constant, it robs people of responsibility."

Ms. Sharma spoke next, her voice steady, calm, carrying the patience of someone used to balancing opposites. "In sales, feedback is a daily necessity. Targets move, clients change their minds, pitches evolve. But here's the thing: not all feedback can be instant. Some things need time to play out. A sales strategy may look weak in week one but prove strong in month three. If I interfere too early, I might kill a seed before it sprouts."

She offered a faint smile. "What frustrates me is the expectation that every task, every meeting, every line deserves instant commentary. Sometimes the best feedback is patience; the trust that your work will show results without constant supervision. But when I don't comment immediately, I'm accused of being absent. That's the tension I live with every day."

Her words struck a balance. Even Meera, who had railed against silence, looked like she was considering the possibility that waiting could itself be a form of respect.

Finally, Ms. Thomas spoke, her voice calm but firm. "In communications, words are everything. If I gave feedback on every draft instantly, my team would never learn to edit themselves. I once had a junior who expected line-by-line corrections on every email. At first, I obliged. But after a while, I realised she wasn't thinking critically anymore, she was waiting for me to think for her. That's when I pulled back."

She paused, letting the point settle. "Feedback is not about holding your hand through every step. It's about building the muscle so you don't need me later. Too much feedback weakens that muscle. And when managers resist giving it constantly, it isn't neglect, it's strategy."

The audience shifted, processing the nuance. Some nodded, others frowned. Aarav shook his head, but Kabir scribbled something in his notebook.

"What I hear from you is this: feedback isn't free. It costs time, energy, and sometimes even capability. You're not against giving it; you're against giving it endlessly. Because endless feedback can turn into micromanagement, and micromanagement breaks both trust and autonomy." I spoke into the microphone.

"We've heard the hunger for feedback. We've heard the fatigue. Now I want to hear from you. How has feedback shaped your careers—for better, or for worse?" I asked those in the audience.

Hands went up immediately. The tension in the hall told me this was not a theoretical question for anyone.

A man in his fifties spoke first, his voice calm but tinged with memory. "When I was younger, feedback was rare. You waited all year for appraisal day. I remember spending twelve months chasing numbers only to be told, in thirty minutes, that I had 'room to improve.' That phrase haunted me because nobody explained what it meant. Feedback that comes too late is cruelty disguised as formality."

He paused. "If I could change one thing in my career, it would be that. I wish my managers had told me sooner, so I could actually improve instead of carrying a vague label for a year."

From the front row, a young woman raised her hand. "I joined a start-up right out of college. Every day, my manager dropped comments on my designs; sometimes in Slack, sometimes directly in Figma. At first, it was exhausting. But over time, I realised I was learning ten times faster than my peers at bigger firms. Daily feedback turned me from a beginner into a confident designer in one year. Yes, it was intense, but it was growth. Without it, I'd still be stuck second-guessing myself."

Another hand rose—late thirties, a sales manager with tired eyes. "In my team, I tried to give frequent feedback. But after a while, I noticed my people were performing for me, not for the client. They wanted to impress me in reviews instead of chasing real outcomes. I had to step back. Too much feedback shifted their focus from the game to the scoreboard."

That line earned thoughtful nods. Even Meera, who demanded feedback in real time, tilted her head, acknowledging the point.

At the back, a nervous young man stood, still in his induction year. "I joined just six months ago. In training, we got constant feedback, sometimes too much. Every mistake was corrected instantly. It felt harsh at first, but I improved quickly. Then the training ended. In my role now, nobody says anything. I don't know if I'm doing well or failing quietly. Honestly, the silence feels worse than the harsh words."

After listening to those in the audience as well, I came up with one conclusion. "Feedback can be both positive and negative. Too late, and it's useless. Too frequent and it's suffocating. Too vague, and it's hollow. But when it's timely, specific and fair, it changes lives. The question is not whether we need feedback. We all do. But the real question is: how do we give enough to fuel growth, without turning it into a drip-feed of dependency? How do we make it continuous without making it constant?"

"Think of feedback like water. Too little, and the plant wilts. Too much, and the roots drown. What we need is the right rhythm—the right loop."

I drew a circle on my notepad and held it up briefly for the front rows to see.

"The old model was an annual loop. Once a year, the wheel turned, and you got your verdict. Too slow. The new model is a constant drip. Every hour, every day, pings, comments, emojis. Too much. What we need instead are micro-feedback loops. Not annual. Not constant. But continuous enough to guide, spaced enough to breathe."

I looked toward the Gen Z panel. "That means you don't have to wait a year to know where you stand. But it also means your manager doesn't need to hover over your every move. Weekly check-ins. Mid-project reviews. Quick acknowledgments in real time, but balanced with trust that you can figure things out on your own."

Mrs. Nair leaned into her mic. "So feedback becomes less like a report card and more like a compass."

"Exactly," I replied. "A compass doesn't tell you every step to take. It just makes sure you're not heading south when you want to go north. That's the role of feedback."

I glanced back at the managers' side. "And here's another truth. Feedback is not just the manager's job anymore. In healthy organisations, feedback flows sideways and upward too. Colleagues give each other quick notes. Juniors give managers input. The responsibility is shared, not dumped."

I paused and added, "But there's one condition. Feedback must be specific and fair. Vague praise, 'good job,' is sugar. It feels nice, but it doesn't build muscle. Sharp but delayed criticism, 'you failed last quarter,' is poison. It hurts but doesn't help. The healthiest feedback is timely, clear, and actionable. Like protein, it fuels growth."

Mr. Mehra chuckled softly at that metaphor, and a ripple of laughter ran through the audience. The tension lightened just enough for the point to land.

I leaned back, letting my final words hang. "So if loyalty was about redefining value exchange, and hierarchy about redefining respect, then feedback is about redefining rhythm. From annual verdicts to micro-loops.

From silence to signals. From scorekeeping to compass-keeping."

The stories were clear: feedback can build confidence, or it can break it. It can fuel growth, or it can create dependency. What matters is not whether we give it, but how and how often.

For Leaders

- **Move from annual to micro-loops.** Replace yearly verdicts with regular, smaller check-ins.
- **Make it specific.** Praise effort, but point to outcomes. Vague words encourage confusion, not improvement.
- **Balance recognition with trust.** Acknowledge good work, then step back and let people run.
- **Share the load.** Encourage peer feedback so managers are not the only source.

For Gen Z

- **Don't mistake silence for rejection.** Sometimes trust shows up as space, not constant commentary.
- **Ask better questions.** Instead of "How did I do?" try "What one thing could I do better next time?"
- **Build self-feedback.** Reflect before you seek validation. Growth comes from inner scorecards as well as external ones.
- **Respect timing**. Not every task needs immediate input. Some seeds need time to sprout before they're judged.

As the session wound up, I looked at the two panels and then the audience. "Loyalty, hierarchy, feedback, we've redefined those. But talking about just these topics doesn't end the tension. Once people feel seen, and once they feel heard, a new question arises: How much work are we allowed to take?"

"Tomorrow," I continued, "we'll open the most personal conversation yet. Not about careers or systems, but about life itself. The work-life dilemma. Should work fit into life or should life fit into work?"

I closed my folder and said, "Rest well tonight. You'll need it."

CHAPTER FIVE

THE WORK–LIFE DILEMMA

Day 3 began differently. The air in the convention center felt heavier, quieter. The earlier sessions on loyalty, hierarchy, and feedback had stirred arguments, but this next topic wasn't just professional; it was deeply personal.

In the lobby, I overheard snippets of conversation that told me as much.

A young voice said, "If I don't protect my weekends, I'll burn out before thirty."

An older one replied, "When I was your age, weekends were when the real work got done."

This wasn't about systems or processes anymore. This was about life itself; how much of it belonged to work, and how much we were willing to claim for ourselves.

When we stepped back into the hall, the atmosphere was different. The Gen Z panel was sharper, almost defensive. Riya seemed most alert today—as if this was the conversation she had been waiting for. Aarav slouched in his chair, but his eyes gave away the eagerness to spar. Meera had already opened her laptop, fingers resting on the keyboard like a pianist before a performance. Kabir leaned back as usual, but his expression was thoughtful, not detached.

On the managers' side, Mr. Kapoor rubbed his forehead as though he could already feel the weight of what was coming. Mr. Desai adjusted his glasses, his face set in firm lines. Ms. Sharma sat upright, expression calm but resolute, as if preparing to remind the hall of the discipline she believed in. Ms. Thomas stacked her notes carefully, her posture straight, her eyes sharp.

The audience carried its own tension. The younger delegates looked eager, almost impatient, as though this was the session that truly spoke to their everyday struggles. The older executives looked skeptical, some already whispering about "entitlement" before the lights dimmed.

I leaned into the microphone. "Over the last two days, we've spoken of loyalty, hierarchy, and feedback. But today, we step into something more personal. Something that doesn't just shape careers; it shapes lives."

I paused, letting the quiet deepen. "The question before us is this: *Should work fit into life, or should life fit into work?*"

A ripple moved through the hall. Some Gen Z delegates leaned forward immediately. Some managers shifted in their seats. Everyone knew this wasn't an abstract question; it was a negotiation they lived every single day.

I glanced at the panels, then back at the audience. "This isn't about balance alone. It's about meaning, energy, and how far we let our careers define who we are. And I can promise you, this one will not be easy."

The silence that followed wasn't just anticipation. It was personal.

"When I was growing up in corporate India," I began, "work-life balance was a phrase nobody used. The assumption was simple: work first, everything else second. Long hours were not just expected; they were celebrated. The person who left last was called dedicated. The one who left early was whispered about."

I could see older managers in the audience nodding, some even smiling faintly at the memory of their own late nights in fluorescent-lit offices.

"That was the **old model**. Loyalty meant presence. Tenure was measured in hours spent at your desk. Your credibility grew with every late-night email and every sacrificed weekend. The promise was clear: if you worked long enough and hard enough, rewards would come. The price? Family dinners missed, health compromised, lives postponed."

I shifted my gaze toward the younger rows. "And then came the **new model.** This generation has grown up in a different world. Technology blurred the boundary between office and home. You can work anywhere, anytime, which means you can also refuse to work everywhere, all the time. For Gen Z, balance isn't a luxury. It's survival. Flexibility is not a perk; it's a baseline expectation. Hybrid models, remote options, wellness days… these are not privileges in their vocabulary. They are rights."

I gestured toward the Gen Z panel. Riya gave a small, quiet nod, her expression firm.

"But here lies the clash," I continued. "For managers, flexibility often feels like risk. *If people work from home, how do I know they're accountable? If they leave early, how do I know they're committed? For Gen Z, inflexibility feels like exploitation. If I give my best in six hours, why should I stay for ten? If outcomes are delivered, why does presence matter?"*

I paused, scanning the hall. The tension was palpable.

"The truth is, both models carry wisdom, and both carry dangers. Long hours built resilience and stability, yes. But they also burned people out. Flexibility fuels creativity and wellbeing, yes. But it can also erode discipline if handled carelessly. The challenge before us is not to pick one over the other. It's to find a new balance; one measured not by hours or location, but by outcomes."

Mrs. Nair leaned into her microphone. "So the real question isn't where or *how long* we work. It's *how we measure contribution.*"

Mr. Mehra added, "And whether we can trust outcomes enough to let go of control."

I nodded. "Exactly. Work-life balance is not about less work or more work. It's about reshaping the contract: work should fit into life, not swallow it. But life must also make room for responsibility. If we want balance, it has to be earned on both sides."

I turned back to the Gen Z panel. "With that, let's hear from you. What does balance or the lack of it look like in your world?"

The room leaned forward. It was time for the younger voices to make the case.

Aarav leaned forward, sneaker tapping against the floor like a drumbeat.

"I worked in a fintech start-up. The unspoken rule was simple: if you weren't online at 11 p.m., you weren't serious. Slack messages came at midnight. Emails at two in the morning. And the next day, we'd all joke about being zombies. Everyone called it 'hustle culture.' I called it exploitation."

His tone sharpened. "I delivered my projects in half the time. But because I logged off at ten, I was told I wasn't committed. That's when I realised: some managers don't want outcomes. They want control. They measure loyalty by exhaustion. That's not balance. That's glorified burnout."

"I come from a family where my parents gave everything to their jobs. Late nights, missed birthdays, postponed vacations. They told me it was noble. But what I saw was tired faces, missed memories, and a sense that life was always on hold. I promised myself I wouldn't repeat that." Meera said with a hint of sadness in her eyes.

Her voice steadied.

"In my first agency role, I asked for flexible hours. The answer was no. They said clients wouldn't respect boundaries. But when I switched to a smaller start-up that allowed hybrid work, my productivity doubled. I could take care of my health, learn new skills, and still deliver. Balance didn't make me lazier, it made me better."

The audience stirred. Ms. Sharma jotted something in her notes, thoughtful.

Riya, who had been quiet through Aarav and Meera's stories, finally leaned forward. "For me, balance isn't a privilege, it's survival. I once had a manager who measured dedication by late nights. I worked myself to the edge to prove I belonged. One evening, I fainted at my desk. My body gave me feedback before my manager ever did."

The hall went very still.

"I learned the hard way: if you don't set boundaries, no one will set them for you. Now I draw my lines clearly. I deliver, I commit, but I also protect my life outside work. Because if I burn out, nobody benefits; not me, not the company. Balance is not selfish. It's responsible."

Even some of the older managers nodded quietly at her words.

Kabir adjusted his glasses, his tone calm but weighty. "I see balance differently. For me, work and life aren't enemies; they're partners. I want my work to mean something, to fit into my values, my ambitions. But if work demands everything—every evening, every weekend—then where do I build my own ideas? Where do I create?"

He paused.

"In my last job, I was building a start-up on the side. Not because I didn't care about my role, but because I needed a place to pour my creativity. My manager called it a distraction. I called it balance; one part of me for the company, one part for myself. Without that space, I would have felt trapped. Work can't be my whole life. It has to leave room for who I am outside it."

The hall buzzed, leaving some impressed, others skeptical. But Kabir's words carried a quiet conviction that was hard to dismiss.

Listening to them, I didn't just hear rebellion. I heard survival, legacy, responsibility, and ambition.

"What you've shown us is that balance isn't indulgence. It's a necessity. Without it, you burn out. With it, you thrive. But here's the tension: what feels like balance to you often looks like risk to those who manage you. And that's what we'll hear now."

I turned to the right side of the stage. The Gen Z had spoken of survival, creativity, and boundaries. Now it was time for those people who had built their entire careers on sacrifice: the managers.

"When I hear 'work-life balance,' I feel conflicted. I don't deny its importance. But I also know what it takes to build credibility. I've stayed overnight in factories when shipments were delayed. I've missed weddings, birthdays, and holidays because machines don't care about balance; they care about deadlines. If I had walked away at six every evening, I wouldn't have survived fifteen years in this industry." Mr. Kapoor began.

He leaned forward, his voice sharpening.

"Discipline matters. Presence matters. Long hours aren't always exploitation; they're sometimes the only way to prove reliability when the stakes are high. I respect flexibility, but I worry: if everyone prioritises balance all the time, who will hold the line when things go wrong?"

Mr. Desai adjusted his glasses and spoke with the authority of someone who had lived through corporate shifts.

"I've seen balance discussed in every HR meeting for the last decade. But let me tell you this: accountability does not shrink just because personal life grows louder.

A client doesn't care if you had a tough week. A deadline doesn't move because you needed balance."

His tone grew firmer.

"In my time, we were taught that hard work builds trust. Staying late wasn't about glorifying exhaustion; it was about proving that you were dependable. Today, I sometimes feel younger colleagues confuse balance with exemption. They want flexibility without accountability. That equation doesn't work."

The words carried weight. Even Meera, who had spoken about rejecting her parents' exhaustion, tightened her lips at the sting of his message.

"In sales, clients don't wait for our balance. Calls come at odd hours, deals close on weekends, and negotiations stretch late into the night. My team knows this. We don't do it every day, but when crunch time comes, we commit fully. That's what credibility means."

She softened slightly, her voice gentler now.

"I don't dismiss Gen Z's need for balance. But I also know that careers are not built on comfort. They are built on resilience. If you always choose balance, you risk stagnation. The art is knowing when to stretch and when to step back. But if you only ever step back, the rope will slip from your hands."

Finally, Ms. Thomas spoke, her tone deliberate, almost surgical.

"In communications, balance is a luxury I rarely had. Crises don't clock out at six. A bad headline can break at midnight. And in those moments, you need people who will show up no matter what."

She paused, letting the words hang. "I admire Gen Z's courage to demand boundaries. But here's what worries me: sometimes the loudest calls for balance ignore the weight managers carry. When juniors log off, it's managers who stay to finish the job. Balance cannot come at the cost of leaving others behind."

Her voice softened slightly. "What I ask is simple: balance, yes. But with accountability. Respect your time, but respect the team too. If everyone walks away at once, someone has to stay behind. And often, it's us."

The hall was very quiet. The managers' words didn't erase the Gen Z stories; they complicated them, grounding them in sacrifice and responsibility.

I looked across the two panels and then finally at the audience, who had a mixed bag of expressions and were torn between the words of the Gen Z and the managers.

"We've heard the hunger for balance, and we've heard the fear of losing discipline. We are not here to take a side as to who is right and who is not. We are here to listen to each other's stories and problems and come to a common ground."

A man in his late forties stood, his badge swinging against his shirt pocket. "I spent nineteen years in one company. I was proud of never missing a deadline. But I also missed my daughter's first school play, my father's last Diwali, and too many dinners to count. At the time, I told myself it was a sacrifice for stability. Now I wonder if I confused sacrifice with loyalty. Looking back, I would have traded some promotions for presence at home."

His voice cracked slightly at the end. The hall went very quiet. Even Aarav stopped tapping his foot.

A woman in her late twenties spoke next, voice firm but tinged with frustration. "In my last role, I fought hard for flexible work policies. The managers resisted, saying accountability would suffer. But when we finally implemented hybrid schedules, productivity actually went up. Absenteeism dropped. People were happier. Balance didn't kill discipline; it built trust. Sometimes I think managers underestimate how much people can give when they feel respected."

Another hand went up, this time from a man in his thirties with tired eyes. "I manage a sales team. I get the importance of balance. But here's the problem: clients don't care. They'll call at 9 p.m., and they'll demand numbers on Sunday mornings. If I say no, I risk losing business. If I say yes, I burn out my team. I live in the middle of this storm—trying to protect my people while keeping clients happy. Balance isn't just a personal choice. It's a negotiation with forces outside our control."

His honesty drew nods even from both panels.

From the back row, a woman in her early thirties raised her hand. "I run a small start-up. At first, I promised myself I'd never glorify late nights. But the truth? During crunch weeks, I needed my team at odd hours. What I learned is this: balance doesn't mean avoiding intensity. It means balancing seasons. There are sprints where everyone stretches. But there must also be recovery; time to breathe, time to live. Without recovery, sprints turn into marathons nobody finishes."

Finally, a voice rose from the very back. A young graduate, barely a few months into his career. "My manager keeps telling me, 'This is the time to grind. You can have balance later.' But I don't know if I'll survive long enough to reach that later. I want to work hard, but I also want to live now. My fear is that if I follow the old model, there may be nothing left of me outside of work."

His words landed heavily. The hall was silent, the weight of his honesty pulling even the most seasoned leaders into reflection.

"Balance is not a one-size-fits-all answer. For some, sacrifice built stability. For others, flexibility built trust. For some, client demands made balance impossible. For others, designing seasons of intensity and rest made it sustainable. And for the youngest voices, balance is not something to postpone; it's something to claim now."

I looked at both panels. "So perhaps the real challenge is not whether *balance should exist?* But *how do we design a balance that honors both responsibility and humanity?"*

I leaned back in my chair, letting the audience's stories linger in the air: the engineer who missed a lifetime of moments, the HR professional who fought for flexibility, the sales manager stuck between clients and his team, the start-up founder who spoke of seasons, the young graduate worried he wouldn't survive "later."

"This," I said slowly, "is the heart of our dilemma. Work-life balance is not just a policy. It's a question of identity. Who do we allow ourselves to be outside of our jobs? And how much of ourselves are we willing to give away to be seen as credible?"

I paused, then drew two columns in my notebook.

The Old Model:

Work fits first. Life fits around it. Long hours = dedication. Presence = accountability. Stability was built, but the price was exhaustion.

The New Model:

Life fits first. Work fits around it. Flexibility = trust. Output matters more than hours. Creativity was fueled, but the risk was inconsistency.

I held the notebook up for the front rows. "The truth is, neither model survives alone. Work will always demand intensity sometimes. Life will always demand space sometimes. The art is learning how to design both."

I leaned forward, lowering my voice slightly. "Think of balance not as a daily equation, but as seasons. There are seasons when work stretches you: product launches, audits, crises, client escalations. In those moments, the team must stretch together. But there must also be seasons of recovery: downtime, flexible weeks, space to rebuild energy. If we live only in stretch, we break. If we live only in rest, we stagnate. Balance is the rhythm between the two."

Mrs. Nair leaned toward her mic. "So the contract changes from *hours owed to outcomes delivered.*"

I nodded. "Balance is not about working less. It's about measuring differently. If outcomes are achieved,

The afternoon light streamed differently into the auditorium. Day 3 had already tested us with the work-life dilemma, a conversation that felt more like a confession than a debate. By the time we returned from lunch, the room carried a quieter intensity—as though people knew the next subject would cut even deeper.

When I took my seat at the center of the stage, I glanced to my left. The Gen Z panel was visibly animated. On the managers' side, the mood was more guarded.

The audience was equally split. The younger rows buzzed with curiosity, leaning forward in their seats. The older delegates looked skeptical, some already muttering about "romanticising work" before the lights dimmed.

"We spoke about how we work, but we haven't yet talked about why we work. Both Gen Z and Managers have different points of view as to why they work, and sometimes these differences do create a clash." I said.

"The question is simple: Is purpose more important than pay?"

The question caused a ripple across the hall. The line between the generations was clearly visible.

"For some, salary is the foundation—the reason we get out of bed, the stability that allows us to build lives. For others, pay is just the ticket to the game, and the real currency is meaning—alignment with values, contribution, a sense that what I do matters."

I looked at both panels. Kabir's eyes shone. Mr. Desai's arms folded.

"This is not just philosophy," I continued. "It's a real workplace struggle. Do people stay for money, or do they stay for meaning? Do organisations owe us purpose, or just a paycheck? And can the two coexist?"

The silence that followed wasn't calm. It was charged, like a storm cloud waiting for the first bolt of lightning.

I glanced down at my notes, then looked back up at the hall.

"Let me show you two perspectives, two very different ways of looking at why we work." I began.

The Old Model: Salary and Stability

"When I started my career, the answer to why we work was simple: money. Pay the bills. Build stability. Support a family. Salary was not just compensation; it was survival. If you were lucky, it was also status. A bigger paycheck meant you were moving up in life. Purpose wasn't irrelevant, but it was secondary. You were grateful to have work. You stayed because security was scarce, and salary was sacred."

I noticed older heads in the audience nodding. For many, this was the lens they had built their entire lives upon.

The New Model: Purpose and Alignment

"Now compare that with what I hear from younger professionals. For them, salary is the baseline—the entry ticket, not the destination. What they want is meaning. They want work that aligns with their values, that lets them contribute to something larger than themselves.

They don't just want to earn a living. They want to feel alive while earning it."

I gestured toward the Gen Z panel. Kabir smiled faintly, as though I had just voiced his private manifesto. Riya nodded, her pen poised but still.

"Here lies the clash," I continued. "For managers, chasing purpose sounds risky—even indulgent. *What happens when purpose fades? What happens when values don't align? Do we leave every time meaning wavers?* For Gen Z, working only for money feels empty. *If I give my best hours to a company, shouldn't it at least matter? Shouldn't it mean something beyond a paycheck?"*

The room stirred again. Younger delegates leaned forward. Older executives shook their heads.

Mrs. Nair leaned toward her mic. "The truth is, both sides are right. Salary is the foundation. But purpose is the fuel. One without the other leaves you either unstable or unfulfilled."

Mr. Mehra added, "And organisations that ignore either risk losing talent—whether to competitors with deeper pockets, or to passions that feel more meaningful."

I nodded. "Right. The question is not pay or purpose. The question is how we balance the two—how companies stay commercially sustainable while offering work that feels meaningful. And how individuals pursue purpose without neglecting the realities of life."

I looked across the hall, scanning both panels. "Now, let's hear it from you. For Gen Z, purpose often feels like the heartbeat of work. For managers, pay feels like the backbone. Let's put both on the table."

The silence grew charged again, anticipation buzzing in the air. Aarav leaned forward. Kabir adjusted his glasses. Mr. Kapoor exhaled deeply.

It was time to open the floor.

Aarav grinned, as though he had been waiting all day for this question. "My first job paid well. My parents were thrilled. But every day I felt like I was just pushing numbers around, making rich people richer. I lasted less than a year. Why? Because money without meaning felt like slow death."

His voice sharpened. "When I moved to a start-up that was building tools for small businesses, I took a pay cut. My friends thought I was crazy. But the first time a shop owner told me, 'Your app helped me pay salaries on time,' I felt alive. That's what purpose does, it makes the long hours worth it. Salary is survival, but purpose is fire."

The younger rows clapped loudly. Some older managers shook their heads, unimpressed.

"I was in a marketing agency where every campaign was about selling things people didn't really need. I got the paycheck, I hit the targets, but I couldn't stand looking at my own work. One day, I left. Walked away from a stable job to join a sustainability start-up. Less money, more chaos, but at least I felt like I wasn't just adding to the noise."

Meera paused, her tone softening. "I'm not saying salary doesn't matter. It does. Rent doesn't pay itself.

But if I'm going to spend most of my waking hours on something, it has to mean more than boosting a quarterly report. Otherwise, what's the point?"

Riya leaned forward, her voice calm but resolute. "I see purpose as balance. For me, purpose is not about saving the world; it's about alignment. I once worked in a firm that preached work-life balance but quietly rewarded those who burned out. That misalignment made me miserable. When your stated values don't match your lived values, no salary can compensate for that."

Her voice grew more personal. "I eventually joined an HR team where the culture matched the mission. We built policies that actually respected boundaries, not just advertised them. That alignment kept me motivated. I wasn't earning the highest salary, but I was proud to stand by the values of the place I worked. That, to me, was purpose."

Kabir adjusted his glasses, speaking with his usual deliberate calm. "For me, purpose isn't optional, it's oxygen. I once turned down a lucrative offer from a multinational because I knew I'd be a cog in a wheel. Instead, I chose a smaller firm where I could actually build, create, and leave my mark. Yes, I earn less. But I also sleep better at night, because I know my work has weight."

He paused, then added: "But purpose doesn't have to mean abandoning pay. What I want is both: financial security and meaning. If a job pays well but kills my creativity, I'll eventually leave. If it's meaningful but unsustainable financially, I'll eventually leave. The sweet spot is where salary supports my life, and purpose feeds my soul. That's the only loyalty I can offer."

"What you've told us is this: pay is foundation, purpose is fuel. You need both. But if forced to choose, you will choose meaning, even if it costs you stability. For you, purpose is not a luxury. It is the measure of whether work deserves your best hours."

I turned to the managers' table. "But for those who've built careers on the back of stability, this sounds not like hunger, it sounds like risk. And that's the counterweight we'll hear now."

Mr. Kapoor spoke first, his voice heavy with fatigue but edged with conviction. "When I hear 'purpose,' I don't dismiss it. But let's be honest, purpose doesn't pay school fees. Purpose doesn't pay hospital bills. Salary does."

He leaned forward. "When I was starting out, I had no luxury of chasing meaning. My father was ill, and my siblings needed support. If I had told my family I left a stable job because it wasn't fulfilling, they would have laughed—or cried. Pay kept us alive. Security gave us dignity. Everything else came later."

He glanced toward Aarav, then added sharply, "I respect your hunger for meaning. But don't mistake it for the foundation. Stability is the foundation. Purpose is decoration unless your basics are covered."

"I spent 22 years in operations. Not once did I ask myself if the work was 'purposeful.' I asked if it was reliable, if it paid the bills, if it built a future. Purpose is a good story to tell, but it doesn't last when salaries stop."

Mr. Desai recounted a moment from his career. "I once saw a colleague leave a stable role to join a non-profit that promised impact. Two years later, he was back, burned out, underpaid, struggling to make ends meet. His heart was full, but his pockets were empty. And he realised too late: passion doesn't replace pay."

Ms. Sharma leaned in, her tone calm but resolute. "In sales, purpose is easy to talk about and hard to measure. Targets are real. Clients are real. Salaries are real. If my team misses numbers, no amount of purpose will protect their jobs. So yes, I encourage them to find meaning, but never at the cost of accountability. Because meaning without results is just sentiment."

She softened slightly, her eyes kind. "I don't dismiss purpose. I admire it. But I tell my juniors: let salary secure your life first. Once your foundation is steady, then chase meaning. Otherwise, you'll collapse under the weight of good intentions."

Even some Gen Z attendees nodded quietly at her pragmatism.

Finally, Ms Thomas spoke, "I've worked in communications long enough to know this: purpose fades. Missions change. Leadership changes. Today's 'meaningful' project can be tomorrow's abandoned campaign. If you anchor yourself only to purpose, you drift when it disappears. But if you anchor to salary and skill, you survive. And survival is not a dirty word. It is the first word."

She paused, scanning the Gen Z panel. "Purpose matters. It inspires. But pay sustains. A company cannot promise eternal meaning, but it must promise timely salaries. That is the contract. Everything else is a bonus."

Her words landed like a verdict.

"What I hear from you is this: purpose is valuable, but fragile. Salaries, however, are non-negotiable. You've reminded us that meaning may light the fire, but money keeps the lights on. Without pay, purpose cannot stand. Without stability, values can't be lived." I spoke.

"We've heard the fire of purpose. We've heard the weight of pay. Now I want to hear from you, the audience. How has this question played out in your lives?" I asked.

A man in his fifties stood first, his voice calm but tinged with regret. "I've worked in banking for 25 years. The salary was good, the stability unmatched. But when I look back, I don't feel proud—I feel tired. I don't remember the deals. I remember the emptiness. I gave my best years for pay, but purpose never arrived. And now, I wonder if I chose too safe."

The hall was very still. Aarav leaned forward, almost as if to say exactly.

Next, a young woman in her twenties raised her hand. "I did the opposite. I joined a non-profit right after graduation. It was full of meaning—I saw the impact of my work every day. But the salary barely covered rent. I couldn't save. I couldn't support my family. After two years, I had to move to a corporate job. The money is better, but the purpose feels absent. Now I'm searching again—trying to find a balance between both."

Her honesty drew sympathetic murmurs from all sides of the hall. Even Mr. Desai, who had warned against chasing passion blindly, nodded in quiet recognition.

Another voice rose, a man in his thirties. "I once chased purpose. I joined a start-up because I believed in the vision. Long hours, low pay, but high meaning. Three years later, the start-up folded. The founders moved on. I was left unemployed, with no savings, and a family to support. That's when I realised something harsh: purpose doesn't survive if pay isn't sustainable."

From the center rows, a woman in her forties stood, her voice steady. "I've seen hundreds of exit interviews. The truth is simple: people don't leave for pay alone, and they don't leave for purpose alone. They leave when one outweighs the other by too much. If pay is good but meaning is absent, they leave. If the meaning is strong but the pay is weak, they leave. Retention lives in the balance."

Her framing earned thoughtful nods across the hall. Even Mrs. Nair smiled faintly, as though she had been waiting for someone to articulate the middle ground.

Finally, a nervous young man stood, his voice soft but clear. "My parents tell me to chase salary. My peers tell me to chase passion. I don't know who to believe. What I do know is—I don't want to look back in twenty years and feel empty. But I also don't want to struggle to survive. I just hope the future gives us workplaces where we don't have to choose."

"What I hear from you is this: purpose without pay collapses. Pay without purpose corrodes. And every one of us, at some point, has tilted too far to one side. The real challenge is not choosing one or the other; it is designing careers and companies, where the two can live together." I began.

I drew two circles on my notepad and let the audience see. One marked pay, the other purpose. In the middle, I shaded the overlap. "This overlap is where sustainable engagement lives. Not maximum pay, not maximum purpose, but a healthy balance where meaning supports the business, and the business sustains the meaning."

I looked at the Gen Z panel. "For you, the risk is idealism—believing that purpose alone will carry you. But without financial stability, purpose collapses under its own weight."

Then I turned to the managers. "For you, the risk is reductionism—believing that pay alone is enough. But without purpose, talent leaks away, no matter how good the salary."

Mrs. Nair leaned toward her mic. "So companies have to build what we might call *commercially sustainable purpose.* Purpose that inspires people while also serving the bottom line."

I nodded. "Exactly. A company cannot exist to save the world if it cannot pay salaries. But neither can it survive long-term if it is only chasing profits without meaning. The organisations that will win are the ones that make purpose part of the product, not just part of the brochure."

I let the thought sink in, then added: "And individuals must find the same overlap. Choose jobs that pay enough to sustain your life, but also carry threads of meaning. You don't need maximum purpose at every step, but you need enough to stay engaged. That's how careers are built without regret."

The hall was quiet, pens moving furiously. Phones rose again, capturing the sketch of two circles on the notepad.

I leaned back. "So if loyalty was about value exchange, hierarchy about respect, feedback about rhythm, and balance about outcomes, then purpose is about alignment. Aligning meaning with sustainability. Aligning pay with pride. Aligning what we do with why it matters."

The silence that followed was different this time. Not tense, not heavy. It was reflective—the kind of silence where people measure their own choices against the framework.

For Leaders

- **Anchor purpose to sustainability.** Don't offer lofty missions that collapse under financial strain. Align meaning with the business model.
- **Speak to values, not just targets.** Employees, especially younger ones, want to know *why* the work matters. Make that explicit.
- **Reward contribution in two currencies.** Salary for survival, recognition for meaning. Both must coexist.
- **Avoid purpose-washing.** Nothing disengages faster than a company that preaches values it doesn't practice.

For Gen Z

- **Don't dismiss pay.** Financial security is not a compromise; it's a foundation. Build it before you leap too far into meaning.
- **Seek alignment, not perfection.** A role doesn't need to carry your entire life's purpose. It just needs to align enough to keep you engaged.
- **Be patient with purpose.** Sometimes, meaning reveals itself over time. Don't abandon stability at the first sign of monotony.
- **Balance heart with head.** Purpose should fuel you, not consume you. Meaning without money is a short candle.

As the session drew to a close, I let my gaze sweep across the hall. The Gen Z panel looked steady—Kabir almost glowing with conviction, Meera resolute, Riya calm, Aarav restless but satisfied. On the managers' side, there was less fire, more fatigue—Mr. Kapoor leaned back in his chair. Mr. Desai's jaw was still tight, Ms. Sharma thoughtful, Ms. Thomas composed as always.

"Today we asked: Is purpose more important than pay? What we found is this: purpose without pay collapses, pay without purpose corrodes. The future of work depends on the overlap. That is where sustainability lives."

I closed my folder softly.

"We've spoken of loyalty, hierarchy, feedback, balance, and purpose. Each step has pushed us further into the heart of how work feels today. But as we dig deeper, another question rises: how do we stay connected, in a world that is more digital than ever, yet somehow lonelier too?"

Everyone began moving towards the exit. There were talks between the managers and Gen Z; how things worked previously, the new trends, priorities, etc. Mrs Nair, Mr Mehra, and I watched them exit the auditorium and walk towards the buffet.

"Each has their own problems and their own perspective, and neither can be wrong. But what is necessary is to bring out a common ground for everyone to work on." Mrs Nair said as we exited.

CHAPTER SEVEN

THE DIGITAL DISCONNECT

The session we were about to begin was newer, sharper, and for many, more uncomfortable—*the digital question.*

In the lobby, I overheard it again, the tension playing out in real time.

A young delegate muttered, *"Why waste time in meetings when a Slack thread does the job?"*

An older manager replied, *"And why trust Slack when one real conversation clears everything in five minutes?"*

Both these questions made me think that there were two generations, and both generations were right in their thinking.

By the time we re-entered the hall, the contrast was visible. The Gen Z panel looked at ease—Aarav scrolling on his phone, Meera adjusting something on her laptop, Riya sending a quick message, Kabir with his smartwatch buzzing faintly. They lived in a digital-first rhythm.

The managers, by contrast, sat heavier, less fluid. Mr. Desai had his phone face down, almost defiantly. Mr. Kapoor leaned back, arms crossed, his expression already tired. Ms. Sharma stacked her notes neatly, the weight of paper a small act of resistance against screens. Ms. Thomas, calm as ever, tapped her pen against her notebook, her eyes sharp but skeptical.

The audience mirrored the divide. The younger rows glowed faintly with screens lit up, multitasking even as they waited. The older rows sat straighter, eyes forward, as if determined not to give in to distraction.

I leaned into the microphone. "We've spoken about why we stay, how we respect, how we learn, how we balance, and what makes it all meaningful. But today we face a new struggle: *how we talk to each other in a world that is always connected, yet often feels more disconnected than ever.*"

I paused, scanning the room. "Here's the question before us: is digital-first communication more efficient than in-person connection?"

A murmur rippled through the hall. Younger delegates leaned forward eagerly; older ones shook their heads almost instinctively.

"This is not just about tools," I continued. "It's about trust. Do emojis replace eye contact? Do Slack threads replace conversations? Do Zoom calls replace presence? For some, the answer is yes—faster, sharper, more natural. For others, the answer is no: colder, shallower, less human."

The silence that followed was charged. On one side, anticipation. On the other hand, resistance.

I looked at both panels, then back at the audience. "Let's step into it—the world of *The Digital Disconnect.*"

"When I started working, communication meant being in the room. You looked people in the eye. You read their body language. A nod, a sigh, a pause—all of it mattered. Conflict was managed not by typing faster, but by staying longer in the room until it was resolved. Relationships were built on chai breaks, corridor chats, and lunches shared. Trust was forged in person."

I could see older managers in the audience nodding, some smiling faintly at the memory of late-night office conversations that had stitched teams together.

"But it was also slower. Decisions often took days because we waited for everyone to be available. One meeting could drag into three. And sometimes, presence became theatre—you showed up, even if you had nothing to add, just to prove you were part of the team."

"Now, compare that with today. Digital-first tools mean you don't wait for meeting rooms. You type, you send, you react. Slack, Teams, WhatsApp—these aren't side-channels anymore, they are the workplace. You can collaborate across cities, countries, and time zones. Messages move faster than footsteps ever could."

I gestured toward the Gen Z panel. "For Gen Z, this isn't just convenience. It's natural. Digital-first feels efficient, transparent, and democratic. Why wait for hierarchy to allow access when a direct message can cut through layers? Why block half a day for a meeting when a three-line chat solves it?"

The younger rows nodded, some even chuckling. The managers' faces stayed still.

"For managers, digital-first often feels shallow. Emojis can't carry empathy. Messages can't replace tone. Speed can create miscommunication faster than clarity. They worry that trust, collaboration, and humanity get lost in translation."

I scanned the hall, watching both sides shift in their seats. "For Gen Z, face-to-face often feels inefficient. Meetings that could be messages. Protocols that feel like delays. They see hierarchy baked into in-person structures—and freedom in digital threads."

Mrs. Nair leaned toward her mic. "So the real question isn't about tools; it's about trust. Can we build real relationships in a world that moves at the speed of typing?"

Mr. Mehra added, "And can we slow down enough, sometimes, to let empathy catch up with efficiency?"

I nodded. "That's the heart of today's discussion. Digital speed versus human touch. Efficiency versus empathy. Connection versus disconnection. Let's see how it plays out in your worlds."

I turned to the Gen Z panel. "Tell us how digital-first works or doesn't for you."

"Digital-first is not a preference," Aarav said, leaning in. "It's physics. A message sent to the right person with the right context at the right time beats any calendar block two days out. Last quarter, our payments flow was dropping approvals during peak hours. We didn't call a meeting—we spun a Slack war-room. Engineers, QA, legal, customer success—all in one thread. Logs, charts, red flags, quick polls. Ninety minutes later, we had a patched hotfix, a rollback plan, customer comms drafted, and a root-cause ticket filed."

He let the moment hang, then added, "If we'd waited to 'get in a room,' we would've bled for 24 hours."

He wasn't done. "I respect face-to-face when we're shaping something big. But for 80% of work? Async wins. Versioned docs, track changes, comments in-line, short loom videos, everyone contributes without the loudest voice owning the room. That's not just faster; it's fairer."

"I grew up in marketing where ideas die in hallways and flourish online," Meera began. "In my agency days, a junior's concept could disappear because it didn't get ten minutes with the right VP. When I moved to a product-led company, the rules changed. We write in public, not on posters, but in shared docs. One page, two charts, three calls-to-action. You share the link. People tear it apart, add data, and tag stakeholders. Good work rises because people can see it."

She glanced toward the managers' table. "Digital makes visibility a design, not a gamble. I've launched campaigns where the thread itself became institutional memory: what we tried, what failed, what pivot worked. A year later, a new teammate can replay the whole journey in an afternoon. Try getting that from a dozen meetings and a foggy memory."

Then she softened. "But I've also learned the cost. Digital can be brutal. Comments arrive without tone. Sarcasm reads as scorn. I once posted a draft strategy and got fifteen bullets of 'this won't work' with no hello, no framing. I almost pulled the plug. A teammate DM'd: 'Don't quit the thread—ask for one constructive suggestion per person.' I did. The next day, the doc changed. Same critics, better behavior. The tool didn't fix the culture, we did."

Ms. Thomas took a note at that line. So did half the audience.

Riya's voice came calm, like a hand on a ringing phone.

"I love the efficiency," she said. "What I fear is the infinite. With digital, the day has no edges. Slack pings at 11 p.m. bleed into 7 a.m. emails. WhatsApp groups sprout like weeds. If we're not careful, work becomes a constant low-volume alarm you learn to ignore—until you can't."

She paused, then offered a story. "In my previous role, our HR team moved to an always-on support channel. Great idea—people asked questions when they had them. But within weeks, my team was answering policy queries at midnight. One Friday, I wrote a simple protocol: 'Channel hours 9–6. After-hours posts allowed; responses next day. If urgent, tag @duty and explain urgency in one line.' We pinned it, modeled it, and backed each other when we stuck to it."

She smiled. "Response time went up Monday to Friday. Burnout dropped. The team stopped flinching at every notification. Digital didn't change, we changed how we used it."

Riya looked toward the crowd. "Gen Z isn't allergic to effort. We're allergic to endless. Boundaries aren't laziness, they're the structure that lets us give our best when we're on."

Kabir adjusted his glasses, speaking with the unhurried cadence that makes people lean in.

"I build products," he said. "Most of my work lives in documents: PRDs, specs, prototypes, comments. Digital lets a dozen minds shape an idea without fighting for airtime. But I've also watched great concepts die because the medium betrayed the message."

A small smile. "Once, I proposed removing a popular feature we couldn't justify. In the doc, my writing looked clinical: 'Low usage, high maintenance, poor ROI.' The team reacted like I'd insulted their child. A week of defensive comments. We were stuck."

He continued, "So I changed the stage. I booked a 25-minute stand-up. I shared customer clips of confusion, the maintenance backlog, and the opportunity cost. I acknowledged the emotion: 'This feature got us early fans. It's hard to let go.' Then I asked, 'If we freed this time, what could we build instead?' We ended the call with three better bets—and the removal plan sailed through in a day."

He looked up. "My lesson? Digital scales logic. In-person rescues emotion. Ship plans in docs. Solve feelings in rooms. Blending the two is not compromise; it's craft."

I watched as more than a few heads—across both generations—tilted in agreement.

As they spoke, a map emerged. Aarav made the case for *speed and fairness*—threads that move faster than rooms, rooms that often reward volume over value. Meera argued for *visibility by design*—docs and trails that outlive memory, with the caveat that culture must shape how we critique. Riya insisted on *edges*—that the promise of digital efficiency collapses without boundaries. And Kabir, precise as ever, offered a rule of craft: *logic thrives async; emotion needs a room.*

I turned to the managers' side. "You've lived the seasons where eye contact saved a project and where a hallway conversation defused a crisis. You've also watched misfires in channels turn a small mistake into a screenshot storm. Your turn next."

Around us, the room settled into that particular quiet that means people are updating their own playbooks. On screens across the auditorium, I could see new notes taking shape:

- *War-rooms for incidents.*
- *Public docs, private dignity.*
- *Hours, tags, urgency rules.*
- *Docs for plans, rooms for feelings.*

The digital disconnect didn't feel like a cliff anymore. It felt like a bridge we could actually design.

I turned to the right side of the stage. "What are your thoughts on this?"

Mr. Kapoor's voice carried fatigue, but also a sting of exasperation. "Digital is fast, yes. But it is also reckless. In my team, one Slack thread spiraled into three days of confusion. Someone misread tone, another jumped in without context, and suddenly half the department was firefighting an issue that wasn't even real. I spent more time cleaning up miscommunication than fixing the actual problem."

He looked across at Aarav. "Efficiency isn't speed alone. Efficiency is clarity. And too often, digital gives us noise masquerading as clarity."

"When I started, you earned trust by showing up. You looked your manager in the eye, and you convinced a client across a table. You can't build credibility with emojis." Mr Desai stated.

He leaned forward, almost challenging the Gen Z panel. "Last month, a junior emailed me a resignation letter. No conversation. No explanation. Just three paragraphs in an inbox. That's what digital-first looks like to me: cold, transactional, detached. If you can't even face someone when you leave, how can I believe you'll face clients when the stakes are high?"

"In sales, no deal is ever closed on a thread. Clients sign because they trust you, not just your proposal. And trust is built face-to-face. Over coffee, over dinners, over late-night conversations that show you are more than a number in their inbox." Ms. Sharma spoke.

She smiled faintly. "I use digital tools daily. But when a client is angry, I don't send a message. I show up. Because in that moment, presence is not optional; it is the product."

Her words landed gently, but they struck deep. Even Meera, who had celebrated the fairness of digital visibility, looked thoughtful.

Finally, Thomas leaned forward, her tone even, deliberate. "In communications, I've seen more damage done by a poorly worded email than by a bad press release. Digital strips tone, nuance, empathy. A simple phrase like 'Let's discuss' can sound like an invitation or a threat, depending on the reader's mood."

She let the words settle before adding, "I admire digital tools for speed. But we forget that humans are not machines. Context matters. Empathy matters. A five-minute conversation in person can repair trust that a hundred messages cannot. Digital may move information faster, but it does not always move understanding faster."

I looked across the two panels.

"So here it is again. For Gen Z, digital-first feels fairer, faster, and more natural. For managers, digital-first feels shallow, noisy, sometimes even disrespectful. Between speed and empathy lies the space we must navigate."

I turned my chair slightly toward the hall.

"We've heard the speed of digital and the trust of face-to-face. Now I want to hear from you. How has this played out in your worlds?"

A man in his late twenties spoke first, voice confident. "We launched a feature remotely with 30 people spread across three countries. Every detail: bugs, fixes, customer updates—happened on Slack. We shipped faster than ever before. For me, digital wasn't just efficient; it was liberating. Without it, I'd have spent half my career waiting for visas and conference rooms."

A man in his fifties raised his hand next. His tone carried quiet authority. "Digital may move projects, but it doesn't move people. I once led a client negotiation over Zoom. Slides were perfect, arguments sharp, numbers solid. But the client hesitated. The deal didn't close until I flew out and sat across their table. One handshake, one shared meal—that sealed it. Digital can't replace trust that comes from presence."

From the middle row, a young woman leaned into her mic. "I work in design. Digital-first saved me. I'm introverted. In meetings, my ideas often got drowned out. But in Figma and Slack, I could share quietly—mockups, comments, and async videos. Suddenly, people saw my work without me fighting to be heard. Digital gave me a voice I didn't have in the room."

From the back row, a nervous but clear voice spoke. "I'm just a few months into my first job. For me, digital is survival. I can ping seniors I'd never dare to approach in person. But I've also messed up—I once sent a message without context, and it blew up into confusion. I learned the hard way: speed without clarity isn't efficiency. It's chaos."

I looked across the hall. "The question isn't *digital or in-person*. The question is when digital helps, and when it hurts. And how we design rules so that we don't confuse speed with connection, or presence with theatre."

I sketched two columns on my notepad.

Digital Strengths

- Speed: messages move faster than meetings.
- Scale: one thread connects dozens across time zones.
- Visibility: ideas live in documents, not in memories.
- Access: hierarchy flattens when you can ping directly.

In-Person Strengths

- Trust: presence builds credibility no emoji can match.
- Empathy: tone, pauses, eye contact carry what words can't.

- Repair: conflict often heals faster face-to-face.
- Symbolism: sometimes, showing up is the message.

I looked up. "The trap is thinking we must pick one. The future isn't digital-only or presence-only. It's blended. Use digital for speed and scale. Use presence for trust and empathy. Know when to switch."

Mrs. Nair leaned forward. "So it's not a replacement; it's a rhythm."

"Exactly," I said. "Think of it like music. Digital is the beat, fast, continuous, keeping everyone in sync. In-person is the melody—the part you remember, the part that makes you feel. A song needs both."

The hall was very still now, not restless, not defensive—absorbing.

"And here's the shift," I added. "Digital cannot be the default. It must be intentional. We can't just ask, *Can this be a message?* We must also ask, *Should this be a conversation?* A resignation, a conflict, a celebration—those belong in the room. A bug fix, a status update, a design iteration—those belong in the thread. Matching the medium to the moment is leadership."

I let the words settle, then closed softly: "So if loyalty was about redefining value, hierarchy about redefining respect, feedback about redefining rhythm, and balance about redefining outcomes, then digital is about redefining connection. Not faster or slower, but smarter. Not message or meeting, but choosing with intention."

The silence that followed wasn't charged; it was thoughtful, reflective, like people were replaying their last Slack thread or Zoom call and asking, Should that have been a room?

The stories, the clash, the reflections—they had all circled the same truth. Digital and in-person were not enemies. They were instruments. The challenge was not choosing one but learning how to play both.

For Leaders

- **Design communication rhythms.** Define what belongs in a thread and what belongs in a room.
- **Show up when it matters.** Celebrations, conflicts, and exits deserve presence, not pings.
- **Model balance.** If leaders flood late-night channels, teams assume it's required.
- **Protect trust.** Use digital for scale, but don't outsource empathy to emojis.

For Gen Z

- **Match the medium to the moment.** Not every thought needs a message; not every issue needs a meeting.
- **Prioritize clarity.** In digital-first channels, context is half the message. Don't skip it.
- **Respect boundaries.** A faster tool isn't an excuse for 24/7 demands.
- **Use digital to amplify, not replace.** Let tools highlight your ideas, but remember trust is built in presence.

"Today, we asked if digital-first communication is more efficient than in-person. What we found is this:

speed needs empathy, and empathy needs speed. Use messages for scale, conversations for trust. And above all, match the medium to the moment." That leaves us with one final question—the one that started in whispers and is now everywhere: side hustles. Are they disloyal distractions, or the seeds of innovation?"

I smiled faintly. "*Tomorrow, we end with The Entrepreneurial Drift*. And I promise you—this one will test every definition of loyalty, ambition, and ownership we've built so far."

CHAPTER EIGHT

THE ENTREPRENEURIAL DRIFT

Day 4 carried the sharpness of endings. The summit was drawing to its close, but the air in the auditorium felt more charged than ever. The first three days had exposed deep tensions. Now we were down to the question that made every manager sit straighter and every Gen Z eye sparkle: side hustles.

In the lobby that morning, I overheard the collision in real time. A young professional, coffee in one hand, laptop in the other, said brightly, *"My side project is taking off—one day it might replace my job."* A manager walking beside him muttered back, *"And when it does, don't expect us to thank you for splitting focus while on our payroll."*

That exchange summed up the storm we were about to enter.

When we stepped into the hall, the divide was visible even before the session began. On the Gen Z side, Aarav looked restless, as if he had been waiting all summit to make this case. Kabir had a quiet fire in his eyes; this was his arena. Meera looked thoughtful, cautious, but curious. Riya was calm, but her notebook already had words scribbled in bold across the page: *freedom, creativity, risk.*

On the managers' side, the posture was heavier. Mr. Desai sat with arms folded, ready to draw a hard line. Mr. Kapoor's expression carried fatigue but also frustration, as though he had cleaned up one too many exits caused by "passion projects." Ms. Sharma looked steady, pragmatic, ready to acknowledge shades of grey but unwilling to let discipline slip. Ms. Thomas was calm, sharp-eyed, already preparing to remind us of contracts, risks, and company IP.

The audience mirrored the split. Younger delegates buzzed with anticipation, some already whispering about their own side ventures. Older executives sat stiffer, whispering words like *distracting, dangerous, disloyal.*

I leaned into the microphone. "In the last three days, we've asked: why do we stay, how do we respect, how do we learn, how do we balance, what makes it meaningful, and how do we connect. Today, we end with perhaps the most volatile question yet: Are side hustles innovation, or disloyalty?"

A ripple spread across the hall. Younger heads nodded eagerly, older ones shook slowly.

"This is not just a generational clash," I continued. "It is a clash of ownership. Does your ambition belong only to the company that pays you, or can it spill into projects of your own? *Are side hustles the future of creativity or cracks in the foundation of loyalty?"*

The silence that followed wasn't polite. It was electric, like the pause before the first bolt of lightning.

I glanced across both panels. Aarav was almost leaning out of his chair. Kabir's hands rested on the table, fingers itching. Mr. Desai's face stayed hard, unreadable. Ms. Thomas's pen tapped lightly against her notebook, precise, controlled.

I let the quiet stretch one beat longer, then said softly: "Welcome to The Entrepreneurial Drift."

"When I began my career, ambition meant climbing one ladder. You joined a company, built skills, earned promotions, and stayed long enough for the organisation to reward you. Loyalty was singular. Your employer was not just your paycheck; it was your anchor. Starting a 'side venture' while working full-time wasn't just frowned upon. It was unthinkable. Divided focus was seen as betrayal. Why? Because companies invested in you, and they expected you in return. One career, one employer, one direction."

I scanned the older rows of the hall. Heads nodded. Some arms folded tighter. This was the soil they had grown in.

"Now, the picture has shifted. For many in Gen Z, a single job is not the whole canvas. It's just one color. They want side projects, creative outlets, and passion ventures. Not necessarily to escape their companies, but to express parts of themselves that a 9-to-5 cannot hold. A software engineer might run a design shop on weekends. A marketer might build an online brand. A consultant might write, podcast, or teach. For them, this isn't disloyalty, it's identity. They see side hustles not as distractions, but as incubators of creativity, autonomy, and resilience."

I gestured toward the Gen Z panel. Aarav was already smiling like someone who'd been waiting for this validation. Kabir nodded slightly, eyes fixed on me.

"And here is where sparks fly. For managers, side hustles feel like dilution. *If my employee is splitting energy between us and something else, can I trust their focus? What if client data leaks into their start-up? What if burnout rises?* To them, side hustles are cracks in the foundation of loyalty."

I turned toward the younger side of the hall. "For Gen Z, forbidding side hustles feels like suffocation. *If you tell me I cannot create outside this job, then you're not hiring me—you're owning me. My ambition is not theft; it's growth. To them, side hustles are not competition with work—they are complements to it.*"

Mrs. Nair broke the silence. "So the real question is not whether side hustles exist—they already do. The real question is whether organisations can embrace them without losing trust, and whether individuals can pursue them without breaking contracts."

Mr. Mehra added, "In other words—can intrapreneurship and entrepreneurship coexist?"

I nodded. "Exactly. We are not asking whether ambition should exist outside work—it already does. We are asking how to hold it. As threat, or as opportunity?"

I looked at the Gen Z panel. Aarav had his hand halfway raised already, unable to contain himself. Kabir's fingers tapped his notebook. Meera and Riya leaned forward, ready to weigh in.

I smiled faintly. "Let's hear it from you first."

Aarav leaned forward, both elbows on the table. "My first manager told me that ambition outside the office was betrayal. But here's what he didn't see: my side project made me better at my day job. I built a budgeting app with two friends on weekends. It never made big money, but I learned to code cleaner, design faster, and think like an owner. The very skills I brought back into work. When managers say side hustles dilute focus, I say they sharpen it. You stop thinking like an employee and start thinking like someone who owns outcomes. That's not disloyalty, that's growth."

Meera opened her laptop halfway, but then closed it again, choosing to speak directly. "I run a small blog on sustainability. I started it because I wanted to write about things I care about, not just client campaigns. And guess what? That blog taught me storytelling in ways no corporate deck could. It gave me energy. It made me more creative in my main job, not less."

She looked toward the managers' side. "Side hustles aren't always about money. Sometimes they're about purpose. If my job can't hold all of who I am, my side project carries the rest. That balance keeps me engaged, not distracted."

Riya leaned forward, her voice calm but steady. "I agree with Aarav and Meera—but I'll add this: side hustles also need boundaries. I once tried to take on freelance HR consulting outside work. It drained me. I was stretched too thin, my performance dipped, and my health suffered. That's when I learned that side hustles only work if you respect your own limits. If they feed you, good. If they drain you, stop."

She looked at the audience. "So no, it's not black and white. A side hustle isn't always disloyal—but it isn't always wise either. It has to be balanced, honest, transparent."

"What you've shown us is this: side hustles are not rebellion. They are release valves, classrooms, and in some cases, lifelines. They can sharpen skills, spark energy, set boundaries, and express identities. The challenge is not whether they exist—they already do. The challenge is how companies choose to respond."

I turned to the managers' side. Mr. Desai's arms were folded tight, Mr. Kapoor's jaw clenched, Ms. Sharma thoughtful, Ms. Thomas composed but firm.

"Now," I said, "let's hear the counterweight."

Mr Kapoor rubbed his forehead before speaking, his tone weary. "I've managed teams long enough to know this: side hustles rarely stay outside the office. I've had engineers miss deadlines because they were up all night coding their own projects. I've had analysts distracted in meetings, phones buzzing with freelance clients. And when the cracks showed—missed targets, sloppy work—it was my job to clean up."

His voice grew sharper. "You call it creativity. I call it risk. Because when your side hustle collapses, you still expect your salary. But in the meantime, the team carries the cost of your divided focus. That's not innovation. That's unfair."

The room was still. Even some younger faces looked uneasy at the bluntness.

Ms Sharma said, "In sales, focus is everything. Targets are relentless. Clients demand full attention. I had a team member who tried to juggle a personal venture alongside work. Within months, their performance dipped.

Missed follow-ups, sloppy proposals, delayed responses. Eventually, they left. But the damage was already done. A client lost, a quota missed, a team demoralised. Side hustles don't just affect the individual; they affect everyone around them. I'm not saying passion projects are bad. But timing matters. When you're responsible for others, divided focus doesn't just hurt you; it hurts the team. And teams don't forget."

Thomas leaned forward, her tone calm but deliberate. "I admire ambition. But let's be clear—companies don't just buy your hours, they buy your attention. That's what contracts are for. Confidentiality, conflict of interest, and intellectual property—these aren't paperwork. They're safeguards."

Her eyes scanned the Gen Z panel before she continued. "I once managed a crisis when an employee's freelance project clashed with our brand campaign. The optics were terrible. The client questioned our integrity. That one individual's side hustle nearly cost the company millions in trust. Ambition without boundaries isn't noble, it's reckless."

"What I hear from you is this: side hustles don't just live in the evenings and weekends. They bleed. Into attention, into performance, into trust. For you, they are not harmless; they are liabilities. And when the line between learning and leakage blurs, companies fear the cost will outweigh the benefit."

I looked at both sides of the stage. "So once again, we are in the middle of a fracture. For Gen Z, side hustles feel like freedom. For managers, they feel betrayed. Between freedom and fear lies the question: can ambition be designed, not denied?"

I looked at the audience. "We've heard both sides—the passion of Gen Z, the caution of managers. But I want to hear from you. How have side hustles played out in your lives?"

A man in his mid-twenties spoke first, his voice quick and eager. "I built a YouTube channel during my first year in consulting. At first, it was just fun; productivity hacks, career tips. But within a year, it was making real money. Did it distract me from my job? No. In fact, it made me sharper. I learned storytelling, editing, and personal branding—all of which made me better at client presentations. My employer saw it as disloyal. I saw it as growth. Eventually, I left—but not because I hated them. Because the side hustle became the main hustle."

From the middle rows, a woman in her forties stood, her tone steady but firm. "I had a team member who started freelancing quietly. At first, I didn't know. But then deadlines slipped. Mistakes multiplied. When I finally confronted them, they admitted they were working nights on another project. That side hustle cost the company two clients and damaged our reputation. I support ambition, but not at the cost of accountability. If you can't manage both, then choose."

A young woman spoke next, smiling with quiet pride. "I started an Etsy shop selling handmade crafts while working full-time. My manager actually encouraged me, said it would spark creativity. And it did. I came to work more energized, with new design ideas. That shop never became huge, but it kept me happy. Sometimes side hustles aren't about escape. They're about expression." Her honesty drew warm applause, even from a few skeptical faces.

A man in his late fifties raised his hand, his tone blunt. "I'll say this clearly. Side hustles are a luxury. In my time, survival left no room for hobbies that might or might not pay off. We were grateful to have one job. I worry that this obsession with side projects creates restlessness. Instead of mastering their craft, young professionals spread themselves thin and leave before they've built credibility. That's not entrepreneurship. That's impatience."

I scanned the hall. "So the real question isn't *should side hustles exist?* They already do. The question is *how do we balance freedom with focus, creativity with accountability, ownership with loyalty?*"

"This," I said slowly, "is the storm we are sitting in. For one side, side hustles are classrooms, fuel, identity. For the other, they are distractions, risks, breaches of trust. Both sides are right. And both sides are incomplete."

I leaned forward, drawing two shapes on my notepad. A circle for the company. A smaller circle beside it for the side hustle. "The problem is not the existence of both circles. The problem is the lack of rules for how they overlap."

I looked toward the Gen Z panel. "You want freedom to build. Fair. But freedom without accountability corrodes trust."

Then I turned to the managers. "You want loyalty and focus. Fair. But loyalty without room for creativity suffocates talent."

I paused, then said it plainly: "The solution is not denial; it is design. Intrapreneurship pathways inside companies, and clear boundaries outside them."

Mrs. Nair leaned toward her mic. "Meaning companies should create safe spaces where employees can innovate within?"

"Exactly," I replied. "If a young analyst has energy for building, give them a sandbox inside the firm. Let them pitch ideas, run pilots, create new value. Channel their ambition inward before you lose it outward."

Mr. Mehra added, "And if they still want to build outside?"

"Then the rule must be clarity," I said. "Declare it. Document it. Draw boundaries. A side hustle is fine if it doesn't compete with the company, doesn't use company resources, and doesn't compromise performance. Transparency turns suspicion into trust. Hiding it turns trust into suspicion."

I let that settle. The room was quiet, but not hostile—just thoughtful.

"So if loyalty was about value, hierarchy about respect, feedback about rhythm, balance about outcomes, purpose about alignment, and digital about connection, then entrepreneurship is about boundaries. Boundaries that protect both the company and the individual. Because ambition will not shrink, it will only grow. The question is whether we build containers for it, or let it leak through cracks."

The silence that followed was softer now, as though the storm had shifted from lightning to rain. People weren't just clashing anymore. They were considering.

The energy was different now. Not combative, not defensive—more like a quiet recognition that the question wasn't going away. Side hustles weren't a trend. They were a reality. The choice wasn't whether to allow them. The choice was whether to handle them with suspicion or with design. So I closed the session with lessons for both sides.

For leaders

- **Build intrapreneurship pathways.** Give employees a sandbox inside the company—innovation labs, hackathons, pilot budgets—so they channel ambition inward.
- **Set clear boundaries.** Define what's acceptable outside work: no conflict of interest, no use of company IP, no compromise of performance.
- **Encourage transparency.** Make disclosure safe. Hidden side hustles breed suspicion. Open conversations build trust.
- **See passion as retention, not risk.** If people feel stifled, they leave. If they feel supported, they often stay.

For Gen Z

- **Build intrapreneurship pathways.** Give employees a sandbox inside the company—innovation labs, hackathons, pilot budgets—so they channel ambition inward.

- **Set clear boundaries.** Define what's acceptable outside work: no conflict of interest, no use of company IP, no compromise of performance.
- **Encourage transparency.** Make disclosure safe. Hidden side hustles breed suspicion. Open conversations build trust.
- **See passion as retention, not risk.** If people feel stifled, they leave. If they feel supported, they often stay.

CHAPTER NINE

THE CLOSING COMPACT

The air in the convention center was no longer tense with anticipation or sharp with disagreement. Instead, it carried the heaviness of everything we had said aloud—and the quiet relief that nothing had been left unsaid.

As I walked toward the stage for the last time, I thought of where it had all begun. An airport lounge, two conversations colliding in my ears. A frustrated executive lamenting Gen Z's disloyalty. A young professional insisting she needed growth, not tenure. That chance moment had brought us here. And now, after four days of fire and fatigue, laughter and silence, we stood ready to close.

The hall looked different too. The younger delegates no longer huddled only with their own; I saw clusters where managers and fresh graduates stood shoulder to shoulder, talking over coffee. The arguments hadn't disappeared, but they had softened into conversations. That, in itself, was a quiet victory.

On stage, the panels sat differently as well. Aarav, who had leaned forward in restless defiance on Day 1, now sat steadier, notebook open. Meera had her laptop closed, choosing presence over keystrokes. Riya, calm as ever, carried the quiet authority of someone who had proven that balance was not weakness. Kabir's eyes still glowed with entrepreneurial fire, but there was less impatience, more patience in his posture.

Across from them, the managers looked no less weathered but less combative. Mr. Kapoor's shoulders carried fatigue, but not bitterness. Mr. Desai still folded his arms, but his expression was less hard, more curious. Ms. Sharma's notes were neat stacks, but she smiled faintly at the Gen Z panel now and then. Ms. Thomas, sharp as ever, had stopped tapping her pen. She was listening.

I took my seat at the center and leaned into the microphone. "Four days ago, we began with a question: can two generations not just talk past each other, but actually hear each other? Today, we end with a different task—not to debate, not to defend, but to distill. To take everything we've argued, confessed, resisted, and reimagined, and shape it into something we can carry forward."

I paused, letting the silence deepen. "This final session is not about winners or losers. It is about a compact. A shared understanding. A promise of how we will work together—not perfectly, but better."

The hall grew very still. The panels shifted in their chairs. The moment had arrived.

"Before we attempt to draft any compact," I said, "I want to hear from you. What will you carry home from this summit?"

A man in his late forties spoke first, his voice measured. "When I came here, I believed loyalty was only about tenure. But after listening to these sessions, I realise loyalty is not just years—it's engagement. I won't pretend it's easy for me to accept job-hopping, but I understand now that growth is also loyalty, in its own way. I'll take that back to my team."

From the middle rows, a woman in her twenties leaned into her mic. "I've spent a year rolling my eyes at hierarchy. Today, I admit I hadn't thought enough about accountability. Flattening layers doesn't mean ignoring responsibility. Respect doesn't vanish with designations—it just has to be earned differently. I'll take that balance back with me."

A woman in her fifties spoke next, her tone firm but reflective. "I came here frustrated by endless demands for feedback. Now I see it differently. Young professionals don't need micromanagement; they need signals. Small, clear, timely nudges that guide, not control. I'll work with my managers to shift us from annual verdicts to micro-feedback loops."

"My biggest lesson? Balance is not indulgence. I used to feel guilty for wanting time outside work. Now I see it's my responsibility—to myself, to my health, and even to my employer. If I burn out, nobody wins. I'll carry that truth forward." A young graduate said.

A woman in her early thirties raised her hand, her voice crisp. "For me, purpose is the takeaway. Pay matters, of course—but without alignment, people leave. I'm going back determined to tie every role in my company to a story of why it matters. Not just tasks, but meaning. Because that's what holds people."

A man in his late fifties leaned in, his tone blunt but softened by reflection. "I'll be honest: I still don't trust digital-first completely. But I've learned not every message needs a meeting, and not every meeting needs a message. 'Matching the medium to the moment,' that phrase will stay with me. I'll teach it to my team."

Finally, a woman in her thirties spoke, her words cutting to the heart of the last debate. "I've always seen side hustles as threats. But today I leave with a shift: they're not disloyal by default. They're energy. The challenge is boundaries. I'll work with my HR team to draft disclosure policies that make ambition safe, not secret."

The room was very still at her words. This was the bridge we had been trying to build.

After hearing what everyone had to say, I moved towards the microphone, "You came with certainties, and you're leaving with tensions. And that is good. Because work is not built on absolutes—it's built on balances. Between tenure and growth, respect and accountability, feedback and autonomy, effort and rest, pay and purpose, speed and trust, loyalty and freedom. Each of you has found a piece of that balance in these four days."

I took a slow breath and let my gaze sweep across the hall. "We've heard final reflections from you," I said softly, "and now it is my turn to tie the threads together. Seven themes, four days, one compact."

I spread my notes on the desk—not to read, but to show the scrawled words, arrows, underlines that had accumulated across the summit. They weren't neat. They weren't polished. They were alive—like the very debates that had birthed them.

1. Loyalty → From Tenure to Value

"On Day 1, we began with loyalty. For one side, it was measured in years. For the other, in impact. What we found was this: loyalty has shifted from tenure to value exchange. You stay as long as both sides are giving and receiving meaning. That is not disloyalty. That is reality. The compact we must build: loyalty equals engagement, not calendars."

2. Hierarchy → From Designation to Respect

"Then came hierarchy. For managers, hierarchy was discipline. For Gen Z, it was suffocation. What we found was this: hierarchy is not disappearing, but it is flattening. Respect will no longer flow from titles alone—it must be earned through competence and listening. The compact we must build: flatten unnecessary layers, preserve accountability."

3. Feedback → From Annual Reviews to Micro-Loops

"On Day 2, we turned to feedback. One side lived by the annual verdict. The other grew up on instant likes. What we found was this: feedback must become micro-loops. Not annual, not hourly, but frequent enough to guide, spacious enough to trust. The compact we must build: feedback is not a report card—it is a compass."

4. Balance → From Hours to Outcomes

"Then came balance. For older models, long hours equaled dedication. For younger ones, balance equaled survival. What we found was this: balance must be measured in outcomes, not hours. Work will always have seasons of stretch, but it must also have seasons of recovery. The compact we must build: balance is responsibility, not indulgence."

5. Purpose → From Pay Alone to Alignment

"The third day, we asked about the purpose. For one side, pay was the foundation. For the other, purpose was the fire. What we found was this: pay sustains, purpose inspires, and the future belongs to the overlap. The compact we must build: organisations must offer commercially sustainable purpose, and individuals must balance heart with head."

6. Digital → From Either/Or to Both/And

"Next, we stepped into the digital debate. For Gen Z, digital was speed and fairness. For managers, in-person was empathy and trust. What we found was this: digital is the beat, in-person is the melody. Work needs both. The compact we must build: match the medium to the moment."

7. Entrepreneurship → From Denial to Design

"And finally, we closed with side hustles. For managers, they were distractions. For Gen Z, they were identity. What we found was this: ambition cannot be denied, only designed. Intrapreneurship pathways inside, clear boundaries outside. The compact we must build: freedom with focus, creativity with accountability."

"All seven debates brought us to the same truth: the workplace is no longer built on obedience. It is built on exchange. Not contracts of tenure, hours, or hierarchy—but compacts of value, respect, rhythm, balance, alignment, connection, and freedom."

I paused, scanning the hall. "This is not just a generational negotiation. It is a redesign of work itself.

And if we succeed, we don't just make workplaces better—we make lives better. Because we spend most of our lives here. And lives cannot be wasted in mistrust."

"It's time to now put it all into words. A promise between generations, leaders and employees. This is what we can all carry back home." Mrs Nair spoke as she pointed toward the screen.

The Compact

On Loyalty

- Leaders will measure loyalty by engagement, not calendars.
- Employees will honour loyalty by contributing fully while they are here.

On Hierarchy

- Leaders will flatten unnecessary layers, but preserve accountability.
- Employees will respect organisational wisdom while earning their own voice.

On Feedback

- Leaders will shift from annual verdicts to micro-feedback loops.
- Employees will stay open to guidance without mistaking it for control.

On Balance

- Leaders will measure by outcomes, not hours.
- Employees will take responsibility for balance as discipline, not indulgence.

On Purpose

- Leaders will tie roles to authentic, commercially sustainable purpose.
- Employees will align passion with performance, not abandon one for the other.

On Digital

- Leaders will blend digital efficiency with intentional human touchpoints.
- Employees will match the medium to the moment—message or meeting.

On Entrepreneurship

- Leaders will build intrapreneurship pathways inside and trust outside ambition with boundaries.
- Employees will be transparent about side hustles and respect focus, IP, and performance.

I paused, then read the last line aloud:

"We will not see work as obedience. We will see it as exchange. Not contracts alone, but compacts of value, respect, rhythm, balance, alignment, connection, and freedom."

The compact lingered on the screen behind us, its lines glowing faintly in the dimmed hall. Nobody reached for their phones. Nobody stirred. It was as though the entire room had collectively decided to hold its breath.

I leaned into the microphone. "When I first overheard those two conversations at the airport lounge, I didn't imagine it would bring us here. But what we've built together is not a debate—it's a compass. Not perfect, not final, but enough to point us forward. Remember: compacts live only if we practice them, not just quote them."

I set my notes aside. "That is my closing reflection. Now let me hand it to my colleagues."

Mrs. Nair leaned into her microphone, her voice calm but resonant. "I've spent three decades in leadership. I've seen reforms, reorganisations, revolutions. But what I've heard these past four days has taught me something my years could not—that listening to discomfort is itself an act of leadership. My reflection is simple: the future of work will not be built by silencing impatience, but by harnessing it."

Her words landed softly but firmly, like a hand on a shoulder.

Mr. Mehra adjusted his glasses, his tone quieter than usual, almost reflective. "When we began, I expected friction. And I wasn't wrong. But what surprised me was the overlap—the spaces where both sides unknowingly wanted the same thing: respect, growth, trust. My reflection is this: if we focus on overlaps instead of fractures, we will find more bridges than walls."

I looked at them both and then back at the audience. "You've heard us debate, reflect, and now close. But the true test will not be here. It will be Monday morning, when you step back into your offices, your teams, your homes. Will you carry this compact as a note, or as a practice? That is the real summit."

The applause came slowly at first, then built into something steady, unpolished, almost raw. It wasn't the polite rhythm of a corporate conference. It was the sound of people exhaling after carrying too much for too long.

I let it rise, then raised a hand gently, quieting the hall one last time.

"Four days ago," I said, "we walked into this room divided—by years, by habits, by frustrations. Today, we leave not united, perhaps, but more understanding of one another. And that is enough. Because progress is not agreement. Progress is recognition."

I closed my folder, no longer needing it. "We debated loyalty, hierarchy, feedback, balance, purpose, connection, and entrepreneurship. We reframed them. We argued, we laughed, we disagreed. But in the end, we found a compact. Not a contract of obedience, but a promise of exchange. That is what we carry forward."

I looked across the hall, at the faces of Gen Z and managers, veterans and fresh graduates, leaders and learners. Some tired, some energized, all changed in small ways.

"And remember," I added, letting my voice drop lower, almost conspiratorial, "this was never just about Gen Z. Because even as we speak, the next generation is waiting. Gen Alpha. They will walk into your offices soon, carrying their own demands, their own impatience, their own vision of work."

A ripple of nervous laughter spread across the hall.

I smiled faintly. "So the real question is not whether we are ready for Gen Z. The real question is—are we ready for what comes next?"

I let the silence stretch just long enough for the weight to sink in, then said softly: "Thank you for being part of this summit. The work begins now."

The lights dimmed. The applause swelled. And just like that, the summit was over.

RECOMMENDED READINGS & RESEARCH SOURCES

1. Deloitte - 2025 Gen Z and millennial survey (online article)
2. Forbes - How Gen Z Is Reshaping Leadership And Workplace Culture (online article)
3. Winning with gen Z by dr. Rajorshi Ganguly (book)
4. Zahra, Y., Handoyo, S., & Fajrianthi, F. (2025). A comprehensive overview of Generation Z in the workplace (online article)
5. McKinsey Quarterly - True Gen': Generation Z and its implications for companies (online article)
6. Managing generation Z by Robin Paggi (book)
7. The Deloitte Global Gen Z and Millennial Survey (Annual Report)
8. Gallup: State of the Global Workplace Report (Annual Report)
9. Gen Z @ Work by David Stillman and Jonah Stillman
10. The Alliance: Managing Talent in the Networked Age by Reid Hoffman, Ben Casnocha, and Chris Yeh

11. Drive: The Surprising Truth About What Motivates Us by Daniel H. Pink
12. Radical Candor by Kim Scott
13. The Fearless Organization by Amy Edmondson
14. The Fearless Organization by Amy Edmondson Thanks for the Feedback by Douglas Stone and Sheila Heen
15. Deep Work by Cal Newport
16. Remote

- Office Not Required by Jason Fried and David Heinemeier Hansson
- Start with Why by Simon Sinek
- The Lean Startup by Eric Ries

17. Originals:

- How Non-Conformists Move the World by Adam Grant Digital Platforms & Business Socialization

Sources

- LinkedIn
- Glassdoor
- Fishbowl
- Blind
- Discord
- Slack Communities
- Upwork

- Fiverr
- Etsy
- Reddit (specifically r/careerguidance, r/antiwork)